Traditional Yorkshire Recipes

To a Yorkshire Pudding

Dusta knaw! Tha's famous,
Tha's etten, all ower't land.
Wi roast beef---an a drop o gravy,
Eee---tha does taste grand.
Thou as a lot o relations,
Of ivery shape, an form.
Like yon haggis---now, he's conceited,
Thinks, he's tekken, t'world, bi storm.
He's in a bag, teed up, wi string,
Nobbut a savoury---wi bits o meat.
Na thee---tha's leet, an fluffy,
An thou can be etten, fot'sweet.

Irene Constantine

Traditional Yorkshire Recipes

collected by Mrs Appleby

Dalesman Books 1982

The Dalesman Publishing Company Ltd.,
Clapham, via Lancaster, LA2 8EB

First published 1982
© Dalesman Publishing Company Ltd., 1982

ISBN:0 85206 701 1

Phototypeset, printed and bound by Galava Printing Company Limited, Nelson, Lancashire

Contents

Cover design by Barbara Yates. Drawings in the text by Valary Gustard, E. Jeffrey and Barbara Yates. Photographs courtesy Flour Advisory Bureau.

Oven Settings

Some of the recipes in this book use traditional descriptions for oven settings. The conversion factors for electric and gas ovens are as follows:-

	Electric	Gas
Very Slow	250	1
Slow	300	2
Moderate	350	4
Hot (or Quick)	400	6
Very Hot	475	8

Introduction

YORKSHIRE has long been famous for the standard of its cooking. It has many traditional dishes which are known the world over—currant pasties, curd tarts, parkins, oatcakes and, of course, Yorkshire Pudding.

A typical Yorkshire meal is substantial and solid. Its chief ingredients probably established themselves when this was largely agricultural country on a greater scale than today. Our predecessors came in from the fells and the moors to demand hearty meals, plain but filling, and then went back to their fields and pastures to work them off again. No mere snack would have served them.

This book contains over 250 of the best of traditional Yorkshire recipes. Many have been published in **The Dalesman**, some being sent in by readers. Others have been gathered from various sources, and may have been printed elsewhere at some time. I gratefully acknowledge all these sources, some unknown, and thank those who sent in recipes and who made suggestions about items to be included.

— **Mrs Appleby**

Favourite Yorkshire Dishes

YORKSHIRE PUDDING

The typical Yorkshire Pudding is made with milk and water to obtain lightness and crispness, and it is essential that there should be no fat in the mixture. Traditionally, it was served with thick gravy, as an individual course before the main course, but is now usually served with roast beef.

1 egg; 4oz flour; 1 teaspoon salt; ¼ pint milk; ¼ pint water.

Break the egg into the flour and salt previously mixed in a basin. Add enough liquid to make a beating consistency. Beat well and leave to stand for half an hour. Heat the oven to 450°F. For small puddings use 2½in. x 1in. size bun tray and put a knob of fat in each tin. Place the tray in the oven until the fat is smoking hot. In the meantime add the rest of the liquid to make a batter. Take the tray from the oven and put two tablespoons of the batter in each tin. Bake for fifteen to twenty minutes, or use a dripping tin and bake about thirty minutes, then cut the pudding into portions.

ELDER FLOWER PANCAKES Three Recipes
Recipe 1.

Make the usual pancake mixture. Get one big flower head for each pancake, shake off the pollen, cut the main stem short but leave just enough on to dip the head into the mixture. Fry the dipped head in the usual way. Add a sprinkling of sugar when cooked. Eat the lot.

Recipe 2.

Half-pint milk; pinch salt; 4oz plain flour; 1 egg.

Sieve salt and flour into a basin, make a well in centre. Drop i egg yolk and mix some of the flour in gently with a wooden spoo Add half the milk gradually, stirring in the rest of the flour. Be till smooth and free of bubbles. Add the rest of the milk and stan for an hour. Whisk the egg whites until very stiff and fold in befo using.

Gather dry, well-opened elderflowers, hold them by the stem, ta sharply to dislodge dust and insects, then dip in the batter and fr lightly in very hot vegetable oil. Sift with fine sugar and hold b the stem to eat.

Recipe 3.

Make a normal soft batter. Cut the elderflowers off the shrub an wash very thoroughly. Dip the flowers into the batter, flowe first, stalk sticking upwards. Put into hot fat in a frying pan. A soon as the batter sets slightly, cut off all stalks right down to t flower part, then continue frying as a normal pancake. Befo serving, sprinkle with sugar. Serve hot with a slice of lemon, whic helps bring out the flavour of the elderflowers.

OATCAKE or HAVERBREAD

These were originally baked on a backstone and the process w uite elaborate. The ingredients, just oatmeal and milk, were lowed to ferment. This recipe gives similar results.

6 heaped tablespoons fine oatmeal; 3 heaped tablespoons flour; salt spoons salt; ½ pint milk; ½ pint water; 1oz yeast.

Mix together the dry ingredients, warm milk and water (not hot) d mix well together; crumble in the yeast, and let it stand twenty inutes. Cook in a lard-greased frying pan, turn when brown and ok the other side.

URDS

1 pint milk; 3 beaten eggs; 1 teaspoon salt

Put all ingredients together in a pan and bring to the boil, stir ll. Leave on a sieve or in muslin for about 20 minutes, when it is ady for use. The whey can be used for making scones.

URD TARTS or YORKSHIRE CHEESE CAKES

½lb curds; ¼lb sugar; grated nutmeg (optional); 1 to 2 eggs, well aten; 2oz currants; ½lb. short crust pastry.

Line a pie plate with the pastry. Mix the curds, sugar, currants d beaten eggs and pour into the lined pie plate. Sprinkle with tmeg if liked. Bake about twenty minutes in a moderately hot en.

JRF CAKES

These were originally baked on a griddle over a turf fire.

8oz self-raising flour; 4oz lard; 3oz sugar; 2oz currants; 1oz ltanas; pinch salt; water or beaten egg.

Rub the lard into the flour and add the rest of the dry ingredients. x to a fairly soft dough with a little water or, to make extra good, e a little well-beaten egg. Roll out to about half an inch thickness and cut into rounds. Bake on a greased tin in a hot oven for ten to fifteen minutes, or until nicely brown.

MINCEMEAT (1)

Take golden pippins pared 2lb
2lb well shredded good beef suet
2lb raisins chopped and stoned
and 2lb currants to it.

Half ounce cinnamon well-beat
of sugar ¾ of a pound,
And 1 green lemon peel sliced neat
So that it can't with ease be found.

Add sack or brandy glasses three
And 1 large Seville orange squeeze,
Of sweetmeats a small quantity,
And you'll the nicest palate please.

(for sweetmeats use candied peel)

MINCEMEAT (2)

1lb finely chopped or shredded suet; 1½lb raisins; 1lb castor sugar; 4oz finely minced blanched almonds; ½ level teaspoon grated nutmeg; 1lb currants; 1lb sultanas; 1lb firm cooking apples; 4-8oz finely minced candied peel; ¼ level teaspoon mixed spice; ½ lemon; 6 tablespoons brandy or rum.

Having washed and dried fruit, cut raisins into quarters, roughly chop sultanas, leave the currants whole. Peel, core and chop apples. Mix all ingredients together with brandy, strained juice, and grated rind of lemon. Put into a large wide-mouthed jar. Place a piece of greaseproof paper, cut to fit and dipped in brandy directly on top of mincemeat. Seal jar with two or three thicknesses of greaseproof paper, store in a very cool, dry place.

PLUM PUDDING

1lb flour; ½lb suet; 6 eggs; 1 carrot (grated); 2 slices bread (made into crumbs); ¼lb mixed peel; ¼ nutmeg (grated); pinch of all spice; 1 teaspoon salt; 2 tablespoons treacle; a little milk to mix; 10oz sugar; ½lb raisins; ½lb currants; ½lb sultanas.

Mix all ingredients well. Put in greased basins and steam five to six hours.

PEPPER CAKE

1½lb flour; ½lb soft brown sugar; 1 teaspoon pearl ash (or bi-carb. soda) melted in a little milk; 1oz powdered cloves; 1½lb treacle (not syrup); ½lb butter; 4 well-beaten eggs.

Mix all the dry ingredients, rub in the fat, add the pearl ash in milk, the treacle and well-beaten eggs and mix thoroughly. Bake in a greased or lined tin in a moderate oven for one and a half to two hours.

RICHMOND MAIDS OF HONOUR

The maid of honour tart is reputed to date back to Tudor England. The story has it that in the early happy days of the marriage of Henry VIII and Anne Boleyn the royal party went for a day's hunting to Richmond. Anne and her maids of honour were served with a particular kind of cheesecake. They found these little tarts so delicious that Anne Boleyn invited her husband to try one, too. When he asked what the tarts were called no one could tell him. So the king declared that they should be called Maids of Honour.

Although these little tarts have such a romantic origin, no one agrees about the authentic recipe. For example, some say that puff pastry should be the base—others say short crust.

But whether it is the authentic recipe or not I am sure that Anne Boleyn would have enjoyed these Maids of Honour on that happy

day in Richmond over 400 years ago.

Pastry:

6oz plain flour; ¼ level teaspoon salt; 3oz butter; ½oz caste sugar; 1 egg yolk, 1 tablespoon water.

Filling:

3oz butter; 2oz caster sugar; 4oz cottage cheese; 1oz choppe blanched almonds; grated rind of 1 lemon; pinch cinnamon; 1 eg and 1 egg white blended together.

Sieve together flour and salt. Rub in butter until mixture resembl fine breadcrumbs. Add sugar and bind together with egg yolk an water to form a stiff dough. Roll out pastry thinly, cut into circle about 3 inches in diameter, with fluted cutter and line patty tin Prick base of pastry and chill for a short time if possible.

To make Filling. Cream together butter and sugar until light ar fluffy. Add cottage cheese, almonds, lemon rind and cinnamo. Beat in eggs. Turn mixture into pastry cases and bake in a hot ov for about 25 minutes.

MUFFINS

1oz yeast; 1 pint lukewarm water; 2½lb flour; ½oz sa ½oz sugar.

Whisk yeast in half water, sieve flour, add sugar; mix yeast an rest of water containing dissolved salt with dry ingredients. Prov knead well, prove. Divide into 2½oz pieces. Make into rounds ha an inch thickness; cook on greased oven plates, both sides even.

BRANDY SNAPS

2oz flour; 2oz sugar; 2oz butter or margarine; 2 tablespoo golden syrup; 1 level teaspoon dried ginger; 1 teaspoon brand ¼ teaspoon grated lemon rind

Melt the fat, sugar and syrup in a pan. Add other ingredients ar mix well. Drop in teaspoonfuls on a greased baking sheet at least three inches apart. Bake in a moderate oven for seven to ten minutes until golden brown. Leave baking sheet to cool on stove top until the biscuits can be lifted with a knife. Roll the biscuits round a wooden spoon handle and leave for a minute to set.

SHROVETIDE

PANCAKES

Pancakes are a very old delicacy, and the custom of eating them on Shrove Tuesday is steeped in history, rites and rituals.

The first "pancake" was probably eaten in ancient Rome! Small flat cakes made with wheaten flour were the most important item served at the great Roman feast called the Feast of the Ovens. This feast was held in the second month of the year, a time when our Shrove Tuesday generally falls, and it seems likely that our pancakes stem from these pagan confections.

Later, when Lent was conscientiously regarded in this country, Shrove Tuesday was the day when the good housewife made sure that all the butter and fat was eaten up before the fast began. This was the day she treated her family to fried pancakes!

In Yorkshire, the first pancake was always thrown to the fowls, and the number of chickens which gathered round to eat the delicacy was taken to indicate the years the cook would have to wait before marrying.

Light Pancake Batter:

4oz flour—plain; 1 egg; large pinch of salt; ½ pint cold milk.
Sift flour and salt into a large bowl. Drop in whole egg, then gradually add half the milk stirring in flour from sides of bowl using a wooden spoon. Beat well until mixture is smooth. Gently stir in rest of milk. Use as required. Makes 9 to 10 thin pancakes if cooked in a 9 inch pan.

For Extra Soft, Rich Pancakes, add 1 tablespoon olive oil or cooking oil to the batter at the same time as the egg.

For Sweet Pancakes, sift 1 level tablespoon caster or icing sugar into the bowl with the flour.

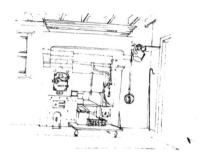

Cooking Pancakes. Using a bristle brush or piece of paper, very lightly grease prepared pan with cooking oil or melted lard, and heat till a faint haze **just** appears. Pour or wipe off any surplus oil or fat. Pour in 2 or 3 tablespoons batter mixture, and quickly tilt pan in all directions until base is completely covered. Cook until underside of pancake is golden, then gently turn over, using a fish slice or broad-bladed palette knife. Turn out, sprinkle with sugar, and roll up the pancake.

N.B.—Avoid using excess oil or fat when making pancakes, as this causes them to stick and break up.

SHROVETIDE FRITTERS (1)

1lb plain flour, rub in a little lard, add mixed spice, a pinch of salt, a little grated nutmeg, ¼lb sugar, ¼lb currants, ¼lb sultanas.

Add **4 eggs, 1oz yeast** and mix to a stiff batter with milk. Leave to rise for two hours. Drop off end of wooden spoon into boiling lard in a strong frying pan and brown on both sides. Drain, and sprinkle with castor sugar. They are eaten warm and can be popped into the oven as required before sprinkling with sugar.

SHROVETIDE FRITTERS (2)

2 eggs; ½lb plain flour; 1oz yeast; 2½oz currants; 2½oz castor sugar; grated rind of 1 lemon and the juice of half; 2 medium sized apples grated; ½oz candied peel; a little nutmeg; about a cupful of milk.

Mix yeast with tepid milk to dissolve. Place in middle of flour and other ingredients, mix and add eggs, then cover and leave to rise, overnight if possible. Fry a dessertspoonful at a time in boiling lard.

EASTER

HOT CROSS BUNS (usually made for Good Friday)

1lb flour; pinch salt; ¾oz yeast; 2 tablespoons sugar; 2oz margarine; 2oz currants; 1 level teaspoon cinnamon; 1 level teaspoon mixed spice; 1 egg; about ½ pint milk.

Sieve flour with salt and spices, rub in fat and add currants. Cream the yeast with a little sugar, add a little warm milk and pour in centre of flour, sprinkle lightly over with flour and leave for ten minutes. Mix to a stiff dough with the beaten egg, adding a little milk if required.

Allow to rise until the mixture doubles itself in size, divide into twelve portions, mould into small buns, mark with a cross and place on a greased and floured tin. Allow to rise until half as large again. Bake in a hot oven about eight minutes. Melt a little sugar in a tablespoon of milk and brush over the buns when baked.

GOOD FRIDAY FISH PIE

1lb of cod or haddock; mashed potatoes; a little grated chees parsley sauce, made as follows:

1oz butter melted in a saucepan, add **1oz cornflour** and mix we Remove from heat and add **½ pint milk**; return to heat and st until it boils; **season to taste** and add **one or two tablespoons** chopped parsley.

Boil the fish and remove skin and bones. Flake the flesh into pie-dish and pour over the parsley sauce. Cover with **mash** potatoes and sprinkle with grated cheese. Bake in a moderate ve until nicely browned.

EASTER SIMNEL CAKE

½lb flour (wholemeal makes a good cake); ½lb currants; 4 sultanas; 2oz candied peel; ½lb soft brown sugar; 6oz butter; 4 eg ½ teaspoon cinnamon.

For the Almond paste: 4oz castor sugar; 4oz ground almon a small egg.

Cream butter and sugar, add each egg separately and stir in t currants, sultanas, peel, flour and cinnamon. Work the grou almonds, sugar and egg to a stiff paste and roll out to the size of t cake tin. Put half the cake mixture into a lined cake tin, add t almond paste and lastly the remaining cake mixture. Bake in a sl oven about two hours.

TANSY PUDDING

2oz white breadcrumbs; 1oz sugar; ½oz butter; 2 eggs; ½ p milk; 1 dessertspoon finely chopped tansy leaves.

Boil the milk and pour over the breadcrumbs; leave for half hour. Add the well-beaten eggs to the sugar and tansy, mix with breadcrumbs and milk, add the butter and bake in a pie dish i moderate oven until set. Eat cold with cream.

EASTER NEST CAKE

Sponge Recipe:

4oz castor sugar; 4 large eggs; 4oz plain flour; 1 level teaspoon baking powder.

Sieve together the flour and baking powder. Separate the yolks from the whites of eggs. Whisk the yolks and sugar till thick, creamy and pale in colour (about 15 minutes), then fold in the stiffly beaten egg whites alternately with the flour. Turn mixture into 2 sandwich tins—lightly greased and coated with equal quantities of flour and sugar—and bake in a moderate oven for 30 minutes. When cool, remove a large circle from the centre of one sponge. Put the remaining ring on top of the other sponge, sandwiching with chocolate butter cream. Roughly coat the cake all over with the rest of the butter cream and then fill the centre with marzipan or fondant eggs and stand a chick on the inside edge of the ring.

Chocolate Butter Cream

4oz butter or margarine; 5oz icing sugar; 2 tablespoons cocoa powder; few drops vanilla essence

Sieve sugar and cocoa powder. Cream with the butter till light and fluffy then add the vanilla essence.

Marzipan Eggs

1½oz ground almonds; 3oz icing sugar (sieved); a little beaten egg.

Mix together the sugar and almonds. Add sufficient egg to bind the mixture into a stiff paste. Shape into eggs. For contrast colour some of the paste pink or green. To speckle the eggs, dot with gravy browning, using a fine paint brush.

WHITSUNTIDE

In many country areas **BAKED CUSTARD TARTS** are a tradtional Whitsuntide treat. For these you will need:

Short crust pastry: 1 pint milk; 4 eggs; 1 tablespoon sugar.

Line a deep pie dish with short crust pastry, pressing it well in. Beat the eggs well and add the sugar, then the milk and stir well together. Pour into the pastry and bake in a fairly hot oven for fifteen minutes, then reduce the heat to moderate and bake until the custard is set (about another half an hour). Make sure the fat is well rubbed into the flour for the pastry, otherwise this will rise to the top of the custard.

GUNPOWDER PLOT (November 5th)

PLOT TOFFEE

1lb demerara sugar; 4oz butter or margarine; 4oz treacle; 1 tablespoon of vinegar; 1 tablespoon of water; 1 tablespoon of milk.

Bring ingredients except vinegar to the boil, stirring all the time. Keep boiling gently for fifteen to twenty minutes, still stirring to prevent burning, until the mixture becomes brittle when dropped into a cup of cold water. Stir in the vinegar and pour into well-greased shallow tins. When nearly set score deeply with a knife into conveniently-sized squares.

YORKSHIRE PARKIN

½lb flour; ½lb medium oatmeal; ¼lb soft brown sugar; ½ teaspoon ginger; 10oz treacle; 3oz lard; about ¼ pint milk; 1 teaspoon bi-carb. soda.

Mix together the flour, oatmeal and ginger, melt the sugar, lard and treacle and add a little of the milk. Put this mixture into the flour, etc., and mix to a stiff batter. Add the bi-carbonate of soda dissolved in the rest of the milk. Mix quickly, pour into a shallow tin 11in x 9in x 2in and bake for about one hour or until firm at 325°F. or Regulo Mark 2.

CHRISTMAS

CHRISTMAS CAKE (1)

10oz flour; 2oz ground almonds; 8oz sugar; 8oz butter; 4 eggs; 12oz currants; 8oz sultanas; 4oz cherries; 4oz mixed peel; juice and rind of a lemon; 1 level tablespoon treacle.

Cream well butter and sugar; add gradually the beaten eggs and treacle for darkening the cake, then fruit, ground almonds, lemon juice and rind and lastly the flour a little at a time. Stir the mixture well and if not moist enough add more egg. Put into a cake tin about eight inches in diameter and four inches deep, make a hollow in the centre of the mixture to keep the top a good shape and bake in a slow oven three and a half to four hours. The oven door should not be opened for at least an hour. Do remember that a too hot oven spoils a cake of this kind; for the last hour the oven should be very slow.

CHRISTMAS CAKE (2)

1lb sugar; 1lb butter; 10 eggs; 1lb flour; 1lb currants; 1lb raisins, stoned or seedless; 1lb sultanas; 2oz mixed candied peel; 4oz glacé cherries.

Cream well the butter and sugar; beat the eggs and add a little at a time. Fold in half the flour; add the dried fruit and peel gradually and fold in the remainder of the flour. Put into lined cake tins and bake in a slow oven for three to three and a half hours. The cake will be firm but resilient if pressed very lightly with the hand when baked.

FRUMENTY

Fifty years ago in the North-East of England, particularly in County Durham and in the Yorkshire dales, a dish of Frumenty was as much a part of Christmas Eve as hanging up stockings is toda and much more so than the still new-fangled Christmas tree wa then in those isolated parts. While the children sat round the fi before going to bed father would bring in the Yule Log and moth would put the finishing touches to the traditional Christmas E supper—a dish of Frumenty.

Frumenty wheat could always be bought in the local shops arour Christmas time. It is the grains of the new wheat, still in the hus

There are variations on the recipe, but the basis is:

Equal parts of crushed wheat and milk and water; soak overnight in a stone jar.

It is then cooked for three hours in a slow oven with sugar sweeten, till the Frummenty is thick and jelly-like.

1 pint milk; 1 pint wheat; 1 pint water; (sugar to sweeten).

The above is a useful amount to make. It can be flavoured wi cinnamon or nutmeg, or honey, and currants, too, can be adde Stir these in just before serving and leave until the currants (if use are soft.

Frumenty is eaten hot, with cream or milk if preferred.

CHRISTMAS FRUIT LOAF

¼ pint warm water; 2 teaspoons dried yeast; 1lb plain flou 1 rounded teaspoon mixed spice; 12oz mixed dried fruit; juice a rind of 1 large orange; 1 teaspoon caster sugar; 1 level teaspoon sa 1oz caster sugar; 1oz almonds, blanched and finely choppe 2 eggs, beaten.

Dissolve teaspoon sugar in water and sprinkle the yeast on to Stand in a warm place till frothy—about 10 minutes.

Sift flour, salt, spice and sugar together then mix in dried fru and nuts. Add orange juice and rind, yeast mixture and eggs, the mix to a dough. Knead well till firm and elastic. Put dough into greased polythene bag and leave to rise till about double its bulk a

he dough is springy to touch. This takes about 1½ hours at average
oom temperature, 45 minutes in a warm place.

Turn risen dough on to a board, knead 2 to 3 minutes then shape
o fit a 2lb, well greased bread tin, or 2 smaller tins. Leave to rise
gain for about 30 minutes, until almost double. Bake in the centre
f a moderately hot oven for 20 minutes, then reduce heat to
noderate 30 to 35 minutes for the large loaf, 10 to 15 minutes for
ne smaller loaves. Brush loaf while still warm with melted orange
narmalade. Serve with fresh butter and Wensleydale cheese.

CHRISTMAS STAR PIE

This recipe has extra apples added to the mincemeat and is
ghter than the usual mincemeat mixture.

**8oz plain flour; pinch salt; 2oz butter or margarine; 2oz cooking
at; 3 to 4 tablespoons cold water to mix.**

**Filling: 8oz cooking apples, peeled and finely grated; 6 rounded
ablespoons mincemeat.**

Sift flour and salt into bowl. Rub in fats till mixture resembles
ne breadcrumbs, then mix to stiff paste with cold water. Turn on
 lightly-floured board, knead quickly till smooth, then divide in
vo. Roll out one half into a round and with it line a well-
reased nine inch heatproof plate. Fill with layer of grated apples
opped with the mincemeat then moisten pastry round edges with
old water. For decorative lid, roll out rest of pastry into a ten inch
ound and cut out a ring of eight stars, about two inches in from
utside edge. Place lid carefully over filling and seal firmly. Arrange
ut-out pastry stars round outer edge, holding them in place with a
ttle cold water. Bake pie towards top of oven at 425°F, or gas

Mark 7 for twenty-five minutes then at 355°F or gas Mark 4 for a
further twenty minutes. Dust top with icing sugar and serve warm
with cream.

YULE BREAD

1lb of flour with a pinch of salt in a basin. Stir **½oz of yeast**
(in a cupful of warm water) into the flour and let it stand for an hour
in a warm place. You need also:

**½lb of butter, ½lb of sugar, ½ teaspoon of nutmeg, ¾lb
currants; ¼lb candied peel; and 2 beaten eggs.**

Cream the butter and sugar, add the eggs and dried fruit and add
to the flour and yeast. Add water as needed to give a slack
consistency. Mix it well and pour into tins. Bake for two hours in a
moderate oven. The old-fashioned way to serve this is to give it
lashings of butter.

YULE LOG

With a wooden spoon beat together **4 egg yolks and 4 tablespoons
castor sugar;** when frothy stir in gradually **8 tablespoons of flour.**
Beat until very stiff **4 whites of egg** and fold into the mixture. Line
a Swiss roll tin with greaseproof paper and spread the mixture about
half an inch thick. Bake in a moderate oven fifteen to twenty
minutes; do not over-cook or it will crack when rolling. (If the paper
is moistened it will be easier to remove). Whilst still warm, spread
with jam or cream and roll up. Wrap fairly tightly in more greaseproof paper and leave overnight. Then cover with a thick coating of
coffee or chocolate butter cream and decorate with a Christmas
emblem.

Soups

COTTAGE SOUP

½lb shin of beef; 1 small onion; 1 small carrot; 1 tomato; ½ small turnip; 2 strips celery; 1oz rice; 2 pints of cold water; salt and pepper.

Cut the meat into small pieces and place in a casserole. Prepare and shred the vegetables, add them to the meat. Add the water and salt and pepper. Cover the casserole with a lid and put into a moderate oven and cook at that temperature for 3 hours. Add the rice and allow it to cook for another hour.

FESTIVITY SOUP

1lb potatoes; ¾lb carrots; 2 medium-sized onions; 2oz butter; 1 dessertspoon sugar; salt; nutmeg; 2 pints stock or water; 3 table-spoons cream; sherry to flavour.

Peel the potatoes and cut into quarters. Scrape the carrots and cut into slices. Slice the onions. Melt the butter in a saucepan, add the onions and cook until soft but not coloured. Add the carrots, potatoes, sugar and salt. Shake the pan well, add the stock and cook gently until vegetables are soft. When cooked, rub through a sieve, return to pan, adjust seasoning adding a pinch of nutmeg and reheat. A little cream, sherry and some freshly chopped parsley may be added to the soup just before serving.

QUEEN OF SOUPS

1lb potatoes, peeled and sliced; 2 medium onions, peeled and sliced; 1 small tin evaporated milk; salt and pepper; 2lb leeks washed and sliced; 2oz butter; 1 chicken stock cube, dissolved 2 pints boiling water; 2 tablespoons lemon juice.

Prepare vegetables, melt butter and fry vegetables gently for 2 to minutes. Add stock, bring to boil, cover and simmer for ¾ hou Sieve or liquidize, return to pan, add evaporated milk, seasoning an lemon juice. Re-heat; do not boil, serve with croutons.

SPRING VEGETABLE SOUP

8oz green peas (shelled); 2oz mushrooms; 3 sticks celery; 4 sma carrots; 1 medium-sized onion; 1oz butter; 1 rounded tablespoo flour; salt and pepper to taste; 1 pint of vegetable stock and mi (about half and half).

Prepare the vegetables, dice them evenly and season. Put into saucepan with the fat and cook slowly for a few minutes, sprink with the flour and allow to fry for three or four minutes, stirri all the time. Add the stock and milk, bring to the boil, and simm until vegetables are tender. If you like the flavour of herbs try **bouquet garni** of two or three sprigs of parsley, a sprig of thyr and a sprig of marjoram tied together in a muslin bag and add when the soup is simmering.

VEGETABLE MARROW SOUP

1 pint water; ½ pint milk; 1 medium sized marrow; 1 onion; 2oz butter; 1oz flour; salt and pepper.

Cut the marrow down the centre and remove the seeds. Cut into small pieces. Grate the onion and add. Melt the butter and add the onion and marrow, allow to cook slowly for ten minutes. Add the water and cook slowly for 40 minutes, then rub through a sieve. Mix the flour with the milk and add to the soup. Stir whilst bringing to the boil. Add seasoning.

ONION SOUP

2 onions; ½lb mushrooms; 3oz butter; 2oz flour; 1 quart stock; 1 pint milk; 2 egg yolks; seasoning.

Slice the onions, clean and peel the mushrooms and chop them finely. Melt butter in a saucepan and put in vegetables. Cook for five minutes. Add flour and dilute with the stock. Stir well until boiling. Simmer for thirty minutes, then add boiling milk. Rub through a hair sieve, return to saucepan and add egg yolks. Bring to boiling point, season to taste.

PEA SOUP

1½ cups dried green split peas; 3 pints ham bone liquor (obtained simmering ham bones in water); 1 onion; Seasoning—if necessary; 1 tablespoon cornflour; ½ teacup milk.

Soak peas overnight in water. Drain, add to ham liquor in saucepan; add salt and pepper as needed and finely chopped onion. Cover and simmer about two hours or until peas are tender. Rub through a sieve and return to the saucepan. Mix the cornflour to a paste with a little of the milk and then add gradually the rest of the milk and stir into the soup. Bring to the boil and serve. A sprinkling freshly-chopped mint makes a good garnish.

POTATO AND CELERY SOUP

1lb potatoes; ½ head celery; 2 onions; 1oz butter; 1 pint stock or water; ¼ pint milk; salt and pepper; chopped parsley.

Separate the sticks of celery, wash thoroughly and cut into pieces. Peel the potatoes thinly, and cut into quarters. Peel and slice the onions. Melt the butter in a saucepan, add the celery and onion, and cook gently without colouring. Add the potatoes, stock and seasoning. Bring to the boil, and simmer gently until the vegetables are cooked. Rub through a sieve (or put into a liquidiser). Return to the saucepan, add the milk, reheat, and adjust seasoning. Serve piping hot, sprinkled with chopped parsley.

POTATO AND WATERCRESS SOUP

1lb potatoes, peeled and sliced; 2 bacon rinds; 2oz chopped watercress; 1 to 2 level teaspoons salt; ½ pint milk; 1 small onion, sliced; ½oz fat; 1 pint water; shake of pepper.

Stew the potatoes, onion and bacon rinds in the fat for a few minutes without browning. Add the watercress and the water and cook until the potatoes are soft. Rub through sieve. Season and re-heat with the milk.

TOMATO SOUP

1lb tomatoes; 1 pint stock; 2oz ham; 1 stalk celery; salt and pepper; 1 medium sized carrot; ½oz cornflour; ½oz butter; 1 tablespoon cold water.

Cut up ham, celery, carrot and onion. Cook in the butter but do not brown, add the tomatoes, simmer for 20 minutes. Pass through sieve, heat stock, mix cornflour with the cold water, add to stock, stir over heat until it thickens.

Savouries

COUNTRY SUPPER for Four

1lb boiled diced potatoes; ½lb streaky bacon cut into small pieces; 1 finely chopped onion; 1 small, chopped green pepper; 4 large eggs; 4oz grated cheese; salt and pepper; a little butter if required.

Fry the bacon gently. Remove from the pan, and in the same pan cook the potatoes, onion and green pepper until very lightly browned. Mix with the bacon and place all together in a fire-proof dish. Fry the eggs in a little butter, place on top of the rest of the ingredients, cover with the grated cheese and brown under the grill.

AUTUMN ELEVENSES

½lb pastry (ruff puff or short crust); 4oz minced beef; 3oz grated raw potato; 1 small onion, thinly shredded or grated; 3 tomatoes; salt and pepper to taste.

Roll out the pastry and cut into rounds the size of a saucer; ½lb pastry makes six rounds. Mix the meat, potato and onion and season together and divide between the rounds. Place a few slices of tomato on top, damp the edges of the pastry, fold over and nip the edges together. Brush over with beaten egg to give a nice colour, make two or three cuts in the top of the pastry, place on a greased baking sheet and bake in a fairly hot oven for about half an hour.

SAVOURY PUDDING

½lb breadcrusts; 3oz suet; 2 tablespoons oatmeal; ¼ pint mi salt and pepper; ½ tablespoon sage; 2 large onions (boile ¼ tablespoon marjoram; 1 egg.

Soak the bread in cold water until soft, drain all water away a squeeze it as dry as you can, chop the suet and onions, beat t bread with a fork, add all the other ingredients and lastly mix w egg and milk. Make about ½oz of dripping hot in a tin and put t mixture in, spread it evenly over the tin and bake in a quick ov about 45 minutes, let it stand a few minutes, and then cut in squa and serve with gravy.

This pudding is generally served with pork, roast goose or du

FAMILY WELSH RAREBIT

3oz flour; 1 level teaspoon salt; ½ level teaspoon dry musta dash of cayenne; 1¼ pints of milk; ¾ teaspoon Worcestersh Sauce; 1½oz butter; ¾lb grated sharp Cheddar Cheese; 6 slice toast; chopped parsley.

Mix flour, salt, mustard, cayenne. Blend to a smooth thin pa with about ¼ pint of milk; stir in remaining milk and Worcestersh Sauce. Melt butter in saucepan and stir in milk mixture. Heat a cook, stirring, until smooth and thickened. Add cheese and p pan over another pan of boiling water and stir until cheese is melt

rve at once over freshly-made toast and sprinkle each portion with
prika or parsley.

ck Rarebit: Serve a poached egg on the top of each cheese
rebit.

GETABLE ROLY-POLY

3 carrots; 2 parsnips; 1 small turnip; 4 medium-sized potatoes;
omatoes; a little gravy powder; suet crust; pepper and salt to taste.
Roll out the suet crust fairly thinly, sprinkle over with gravy
wder. Over the crust lay the grated carrots, parsnips, turnip and
ced potatoes. Cover with a layer of sliced tomatoes, then pepper
d salt to taste. Roll up in a cloth and boil for two and a half
urs. Serve steaming hot with a little gravy.

ASHED SUN-UPS

1½lb hot mashed potatoes; 4-6oz grated cheese; 1 chopped onion;
little butter; salt, pepper and a little mustard; poached or fried
gs.
Cook the onion in a little butter until lightly browned. Add to the
t mashed potatoes, together with the cheese, and season to taste
th salt, pepper and mustard. Spoon some on to each plate and
p with a poached or fried egg.

EGETABLE CHARLOTTE

6 large, thin slices stale bread spread sparingly with butter;
or 4 oz finely grated cheese; 3 small cooked and diced potatoes;
cooked and diced carrots; ½ pint thick, white sauce; 1 egg;
lb cooked peas; 2 cooked and sliced onions; Any other cooked and
ced vegetables can be added as liked.
Grease a casserole or cake tin and coat with brown crumbs.

Line closely and evenly with the slices of bread, buttered side turned
to the sides of the casserole or tin. Keep back sufficient to make a
closely-fitting lid. Beat up the egg and stir it into the sauce; mix in
the vegetables and the grated cheese. Fill the lined mould with this
and cover closely with the rest of the bread. Bake in a moderate oven
for 25 to 30 minutes. Loosen the sides with a knife and turn out onto
a dish. Decorate with piped potato and peas.

EGG AND MUSHROOM SPECIALS

8 slices bread; 1 small can mushrooms (or 2 to 4oz freshly cooked);
4 rashers of bacon; 4 hard-boiled eggs; 2 tablespoons mayonnaise (or
dairy soured cream); salad garnish.
Very lightly toast the bread on one side. Finely chop eggs and
mushrooms and blend with the mayonnaise; season further to taste.
Warm the mixture and spead over 4 of the toasted sides and top with
remaining bread, toasted side down. Toast both sides, the last
lightly, and then cover with halved bacon rashers. Continue toasting
until the bacon is crisp. Serve at once, with salad garnish.

TOMATO RISSOLES—A Tasty Savoury with Salads

1lb tomatoes; 2 teaspoons chopped parsley; 4 to 8oz grated cheese,
according to taste; salt to season—celery salt is good; 1 egg;
wholemeal breadcrumbs.
Blanch the tomatoes and remove the skins. Pulp them down, add
grated cheese and sufficient crumbs to handle. Season with salt and
add the parsley. Add the yolk of egg slightly beaten to bind the
mixture and shape into rissoles. Brush over with lightly beaten egg
white, roll in breadcrumbs with a little grated cheese added, and fry.

MUMBLED EGGS

Heat 2oz butter gently. When it is melted add six eggs, well beaten

and seasoned to taste with **salt and pepper**. Stir gently over a low heat with a wooden spoon. You must take care that the cooking temperature does not increase, as this will make the egg molecules solidify and the result with be lumpy. When cooked stir in **2oz butter** cut into small pieces. Serve with **thinly-sliced fried mushrooms** in the centre and surrounded by watercress.

MUSHROOM CRUMB SOUFFLE

4 rashers streaky bacon; 1 medium onion, chopped; 4oz white breadcrumbs; salt and pepper; 1oz butter; 1 can condensed mushroom soup (10½oz size); 4 eggs, separated.

Cut bacon into thin strips. Cook onion and bacon gently in butter for 2 to 3 minutes. Add to mushroom soup with breadcrumbs and seasoning. Beat in egg yolks. Whisk egg whites until just stiff, then carefully fold into soup mixture. Turn into a buttered 1½ pi souffle dish or straight sided deep ovenproof dish and bake in moderately hot oven.

TRIPE WITH TOMATOES

2lb tripe; 2oz dripping; 1lb tomatoes; a bunch of mixed herb 2 onions; pepper, salt and a large tablespoon of flour.

First cut up the tripe and blanch it. Fry the herbs and sliced onion in the fat, and when lightly browned stir in the flour. Pass th tomatoes through a sieve, put into the stew-pan with the onions, etc and stir till very hot. Add the tripe to the sauce, season and simme for one and a half hours. Chopped parsley and croutons of brea make a good garnish.

POTATO CHICKEN FLAMINGO

1½lb new potatoes; seasoned flour; 1oz oil; 1 clove garlic peele crushed and chopped; ½lb tomatoes, skinned and sliced; ½ pi chicken stock; bay leaves; 4 chicken joints; 1oz butter; 2 mediu onions, peeled and chopped; 2 stalks celery wiped and choppe (optional); salt and pepper; chopped parsley.

Scrape or scrub new potatoes. Dip chicken in seasoned flour, fr in butter and oil for 2 minutes each side, remove. Fry onior garlic, and celery until onion is soft. Place chicken, onion, garlic an celery in deep casserole, add tomatoes and potatoes. Boil stock, ad seasoning and bay leaves. Pour over casserole, cover and cook fo one hour. Taste to adjust seasoning, remove bay leaves, sprink with parsley before serving.

CREAMED CHICKEN COBBLER

1½oz plain flour; ¾lb cooked chicken (weighed after boning

cut into pieces; 1 tablespoon top of the milk or single cream; ¾ pint chicken or vegetable stock; 1 tablespoon Sherry or lemon juice; seasoning to taste.

Scone Topping: 6oz self-raising flour; ½ level teaspoon dry mustard; 2oz butter or margarine; 1 egg, beaten with 2 tablespoons milk; 1 level teaspoon salt; shake of pepper; 1½oz grated Cheddar or Parmesan cheese.

Mix flour to a smooth paste with a little of the stock. Heat remaining stock, pour on to paste, then return all to saucepan. Bring sauce to boil, stirring, then cook gently for 3 minutes. Add pieces of chicken, Sherry or lemon juice and cream. Season to taste and transfer mixture to a heatproof dish, approximately 10in. by 8in.

Sift flour, salt, mustard and pepper into a bowl. Rub in fat and add cheese. Mix to a soft, but not sticky, dough with the egg and milk. Turn out on to a floured board, knead lightly till smooth and roll out to ¼in. in thickness. Cut into rounds with a 1¾ in. biscuit cutter, arrange attractively on top of the chicken mixture and brush with beaten egg or milk. Bake in the centre of a hot oven, 25 to 30 minutes.

CHICKEN GOULASH

4 chicken joints or one medium roasting chicken, cut into 4 pieces; 2oz butter or 2 tablespoons cooking oil; 1 level teaspoon sugar; 1 bay leaf; ¼ pint soured cream; 3 tablespoons seasoned flour; 8oz onions, peeled and very finely chopped; 1 level tablespoon paprika; ¼ pint tomato puree; approx. 1 level teaspoon salt; 4oz mushrooms, peeled.

Skin chicken joints and coat thoroughly all over with seasoned flour. Fry onions and mushrooms in butter or oil very gently till soft but not brown. Move to one side of the pan. Add chicken and fry till golden; 5 to 7 minutes. Combine paprika, tomato puree, sugar and salt and pour over chicken. Add bay leaf. Cover pan and

simmer for 45 minutes to 1 hour. Transfer chicken to warm platter or dish, stir sour cream into sauce and re-heat, without boiling, for 2 to 3 minutes. Pour over chicken.

DOUBLE-CRUST TURKEY PIE

Any cold poultry can be made up this way.

12oz short crust pastry (made with 12oz plain flour, 6oz fat).

Filling: ¾ pint freshly made medium thick white sauce; 4oz grilled mushrooms, coarsely chopped; 1lb cooked turkey, coarsely chopped; 4 rounded tablespoons finely chopped celery (or sweet corn kernels or 2 tablespoons chopped sweet peppers).

Add turkey, mushrooms and celery to the sauce and season well to taste. Cool slightly.

Roll out two-thirds of the pastry and with it line a lightly greased 8 to 9in. heatproof pie plate. Fill with turkey mixture. Moisten edges of pastry with cold water then cover with rest of pastry, rolled out to form a fitting lid. Press edges well together to seal, knock up with the back of a knife then press into flutes. Brush top with beaten egg or milk, then decorate with pastry leaves, rolled and cut from trimmings. (For a festive touch, shape pastry into holly leaves.) Bake pie towards the top of a hot oven for 10 minutes; reduce heat to moderate and cook a further 20 minutes or until the pastry is crisp and golden.

HAM WITH EXTRAS

Some cold ham; a small onion; ¼lb mushrooms; 1oz each of butter, lard, breadcrumbs; a cabbage; 2 further oz of butter.

For four people, carve off four thick slices of ham. Finely chop the mushrooms and onions and fry first the onions and then the mushrooms in the ounce of butter. Drain and mix in the breadcrumbs with the vegetables. Shred the cabbage finely and cook in a little boiling salted water. Spread the mushroom mixture over the ham slices, seasoning well, fold over gently, skewer and lightly fry in the lard in the pan. Drain the cabbage and toss in the melted two ounces of dairy butter. Arrange on a dish with the ham rolls on top. Serve with creamed potatoes.

CRUSTY GAMMON
4lb corner gammon; 6 peppercorns; 1 bayleaf.
Pastry: 12oz plain flour; 3oz butter; 4 tablespoons water; ½ teaspoon salt; 3oz lard.

Soak gammon for 24 hours in cold water. Place gammon in large saucepan with cold water, bayleaf and peppercorns, bring slowly to the boil. Simmer gently for 1½ hours. Drain, remove skin and leave to cool.

Sift together flour and salt. Rub in fat until mixture resembles fine breadcrumbs. Mix to a soft dough with water. Rest in a cool place for 10 minutes. Cut off 1/3 of pastry and keep on one side. Roll out rest of pastry into a large rectangle, 12in. x 14in. and ¼in. thickness. Trim edges and cut into strips 1in. wide. Brush lightly with water.

Stand gammon broadest end down so narrow end is sticking up. Starting at the narrow end, take one strip of pastry at a time and wrap round joint, slightly overlapping. The last strip should just come over the broad end of the joint. Roll out remaining pastry into a circle, dampen edges and place on baking tray. Brush with beaten egg and bake in a hot oven for 20 minutes. Reduce oven temperature to medium and continue cooking for 1 hour. Cover with greaseproof paper or tinfoil if pastry becomes too brown.

To serve, garnish gammon plate with apple rings, and hand apple and cider sauce separately.

Apple and Cider Sauce

4 eating apples; 1oz butter; ½ pint cider; 2 tablespoons sug juice of 1 lemon; ½oz flour; 1 chicken stock cube.

Remove cores from apples and cut unpeeled apples into rings ½ thick. Toss in lemon juice and cider. Melt butter and stir in fle and cook for 2 to 3 minutes. Strain cider into a jug and gradua add to flour and butter. Add stock cube and sugar. Return to h and bring to boil stirring continuously. Add apple slices, cover wit tight fitting lid and simmer gently for 10 minutes.

HOT BACON CAKES
2oz steaky bacon; 8oz self-raising flour; ¼ teaspoonful salt; butter; 3oz strong Cheddar cheese, grated; ¼ pint milk; 1 tab spoonful tomato ketchup; dash Worcestershire sauce; milk glazing.

Remove the rind and bone from bacon and grill until crisp. C into ¼-inch squares. Sieve flour and salt. Rub in butter until mixtu resembles fine breadcrumbs. Add three-quarters of the grated che and all the bacon. Mix milk, tomato ketchup and Worcestersh sauce together and add to the dry ingredients. Mix to a dough a roll out on a floured board to a 7in. circle, brush with milk and into 8 wedges. Arrange on a greased and floured baking sheet in circle with the edges overlapping. Sprinkle with cheese. Bake in fairly hot oven for 30 minutes. Serve hot.

CRUSTY CHEESE BAKE
Five thin slices white bread buttered; 2oz ham, chopped; 2 egg 1 pint milk; 2oz cheddar cheese, grated; 1oz mushrooms, peeled a sliced; 1 level teaspoon dry mustard.

Cut each slice of bread into 4. Fill greased ovenproof dish with

yer of bread, 1oz cheese, mushrooms and ham. Finish with a layer
’ bread. Sprinkle with rest of cheese. Beat eggs with mustard.
radually add milk and whisk together. Pour over bread. Bake in
ntre of a moderate oven for 45 minutes or till golden and puffy.
arnish with a grilled mushroom. Serve hot with a green salad or hot
een vegetables.

HEESE AND EGG PASTIES

**12oz plain flour; 1 level teaspoon salt; 6oz margarine or cooking
ıt; 3oz finely-grated strong Cheddar cheese; 4 to 5 tablespoons cold
ater;
Filling: ½ pint thick white sauce; 4 hard-boiled eggs, coarsely
ıopped; 2 to 3 teaspoons anchovy essence; seasoning.**

Sift flour and salt together. Rub in fat until mixture resembles fine
readcrumbs. Stir in grated cheese. Mix to a stiff paste with cold
ater. Turn out on to floured board, roll out thinly and cut into
venty-four 3-inch squares.

Combine filling ingredients and season to taste. Divide mixture
:tween 12 of the pastry squares, damp edges with water and cover
ith remaining squares. Seal edges and make a slit in the top to let
e steam out. Brush with beaten egg and place on a greased baking
ay. Bake in a fairly hot oven about half an hour.

EVILLED OMELETTE

**3 eggs; pinch cayenne pepper; good pinch curry powder; 1
blespoon water; 4oz chopped ham; good ½oz butter; good pinch
lt; ¼ level teaspoon dry mustard; ¼ pint real dairy cream, single,
ıxed with 1 dessertspoon lemon juice.**

Whisk together the eggs, seasoning half the cream, water, and half
the ham. Melt the butter in the pan and pour in the mixture.
Cook gently, stirring occasionally and loosening the edges, until
golden underneath and lightly set. Brown the top lightly under the
grill. Top with remaining cream and sprinkle with the remaining
chopped ham. Serve the omelette with French bread and green salad.

COUNTRY OMELETTE (for 1 hungry man)

**2 eggs; 1 slice lean boiled ham; 1 small onion; 1/8 green pepper;
1 tablespoon water; 1 teaspoon butter; salt and pepper.**

Dice ham, onion and green pepper. Saute gently in half teaspoon
butter in heavy frying pan. Beat eggs and water until well blended.
Mix in cooked ham, vegetables and seasonings. Heat remaining
butter in pan. Pour in egg mixture. Turn heat low. Lift the edges
of the omelette with a spatula to permit the uncooked portion to go
to the bottom. When it is cooked to desired degree of firmness, fold
over and serve.

WHITBY POTATO WHIRLS

(A good way of using up left-over mashed potato)

**4oz mashed potato; 2oz butter; a little beaten egg; a good pinch
Cayenne pepper; 6oz self-raising flour; grated cheddar cheese; salt.**

Sieve together the flour, salt, and Cayenne pepper. Knead in the
butter and mashed potato, adding milk if necessary to make a pastry
dough. Roll out on to a floured board about 1/8in. thick. Brush
with beaten egg, sprinkle liberally with the cheese, and roll up like a
sausage roll. Cut into ¼in. thick slices. Place on a greased baking
sheet and bake in a hot oven for about 10 to 15 minutes.

Meat Dishes

MEAT LOAF

Browned breadcrumbs; 8oz cooked meat, minced; 1 small onion, finely chopped and fried; ½ teaspoon mixed herbs; ½ teaspoon nutmeg; 2oz breadcrumbs; 1 egg; ¼ pint stock; pepper and salt.

Grease a 5in. cake tin or 1lb loaf tin. Coat inside of tin with browned bread crumbs. Mixed minced meat with chopped fried onion, herbs, breadcrumbs, beaten egg, stock and seasoning. Turn mixture into prepared tin, cover with baking foil and cook in a moderate oven for 1 hour. Serve hot or cold.

MEAT ROCK CAKES

½lb finely chopped meat; 2oz flour; salt and pepper; a little gravy to mix; 1 grated onion; 1oz suet (may be omitted if meat is fat).

Mix, flour, suet, salt, pepper and chopped meat. Add the grated onion. Moisten with gravy to the consistency of rock-cake mixture. Place on greased baking tin in rough heaps. Bake in a fairly brisk oven for about half an hour, or till the cakes are brown and crisp. Serve with thick brown gravy and vegetables as a dinner dish.

BURGER BAKE

1lb potatoes; 1lb lean minced beef; ¼lb mushrooms; 1 large chopped onion; 1 tin tomatoes (8oz); 1 to 2 tablespoons chopped parsley; salt and pepper.

Peel the potatoes thinly, grate and pour off any excess wate Chop the mushrooms, mix all the ingredients together, season taste, and turn into a greased pie-dish or individual ovenpro dishes. Bake in a moderately hot oven for about 1¼ hours to 1 hours. Serve hot or cold with a crisp green salad.

BUDGET BRAISED STEAK

1½lb piece of stewing steak; 3 sticks celery; 3 average slices whi bread cut into small cubes; salt and pepper; 1 tablespoon flou 1 or 2 tablespoons tomato sauce or puree; 2oz margarine; 2 mediu onions finely chopped; 1 teaspoon mixed herbs or chopped parsle 1 pint water + 1 Bouillon cube or 1 pint of bone stock.

Trim excess fat from stewing steak. Melt two thirds of t margarine in frying pan and lightly fry celery and onion, abo 5 minutes. Remove from heat. Add bread cubes, parsley, salt a pepper, tossing lightly with a fork until well mixed. Place stuffi lengthwise down the centre of the stewing steak. Roll up steak a secure with skewers or strong. Fry the rolled steak gently remaining margarine until it is well browned on all sides, about 8 10 minutes. Place roll in an oven-proof dish. Add the stock (water, Bouillon cube) and tomato sauce and cook in a slow oven f 2 hours or until steak is tender. Thicken the gravy with the flour required.

For extra zip, add a teaspoon of paprika to the braising liqui

STEAK PASTY WITH RUFF-PUFF PASTRY

Pastry:

4oz self-raising flour, or a plain flour with ½ teaspoon of baking powder well mixed; 2½oz lard; cold water; pinch of salt.

Mix flour and salt, cut up the lard into small pieces and mix with the flour (do not rub into flour). Mix to a stiff paste with cold water and turn on to a floured board, rolling into a narrow strip. Fold into three and roll out again. Make sure you have one of the open ends towards you; roll always away from you and do not break the air bubbles which will rise. Repeat three times, rolling out the last time to the shape required.

Filling:

½lb minced steak; a small onion, grated; a level teaspoon flour; tablespoon of water; salt and pepper to taste; mixed well together.

Roll out half of the pastry very thinly and line a shallow pie dish. Spread the meat mixture, moisten the edges and cover with the other half of the pastry, thinly rolled out. Press the edge and brush with beaten egg. Bake about half an hour in a hot oven.

YORKSHIRE STEAK

1lb steak; 1 or 2 teaspoons finely chopped parsley, according to taste; 1 medium-sized onion, finely chopped; 2oz butter; 1 pint beef stock; salt and pepper to season.

The steak should be about 1½ inches thick. Score with a sharp knife and rub the chopped parsley and onion, previously mixed, into the cuts. Leave for an hour, season and fry in the butter until well browned. Put into a casserole, add the heated beef stock and simmer in the oven for about two hours.

DEEP DISH STEAK AND KIDNEY PIE

Rough puff, flaky or short pastry (using 8oz flour); 2lb stewing steak; 6oz kidney; 2oz flour; pepper and salt; 1oz dripping; 1 medium-sized onion; about ½ pint water.

Cut meat into small pieces and toss in the flour seasoned with pepper and salt. Heat dripping in a pan, add sliced onion and cook gently until golden and place in a casserole. Put meat into pan and cook gently, stirring until it changes colour and is beginning to brown. Add the water and bring to the boil, stirring. Pour the meat and liquid into the casserole, cover and cook in a slow oven for 1½ to 2 hours. Turn into a 2 pint pie dish and allow to cool.

Roll pastry to an oval slightly larger than top of the pie dish. Moisten edge of the dish with water and cut a strip of pastry and line the edge. Moisten this strip and lift remaining pastry on to rolling pin and cover the pie dish. Trim edges, and press together. If liked, the pie edge can be scalloped with thumb and knife edge. Slit a hole in the centre and use pastry trimmings to make leaves to decorate pie. Brush with milk or beaten egg. Bake in a hot oven for 10 minutes, then reduce heat to moderately hot and bake for a further 20 minutes.

COBBLER OF BEEF GOULASH

Goulash:

2oz cooking fat, lard or dripping; 2 medium onions, peeled and thinly sliced; 2lb stewing steak, cut into pieces; 1 tablespoon paprika; 1 large green pepper, seeded and sliced; 4 tomatoes skinned and quartered; salt and pepper to taste; ¼ pint water.

Melt fat in a heavy pan, add onions and meat and fry briskly till brown. Stir in paprika then add remaining ingredients. Cover pan. Simmer slowly on top of the stove or in a slow oven for 1½ to 2 hours or till meat is tender, stirring occasionally to prevent sticking if on top of stove. No additional liquid should be required if the heat is very slow and the pan tightly covered; the juices from the meat and vegetables produce a rich gravy.

Toppers:

6oz self-raising flour; ½ level teaspoon salt; ¼ teaspoon dry mustard; sprinkling of white pepper; 1½oz butter or margarine; 6 tablespoons milk; milk for glazing.

Sift flour and seasonings. Rub in fat and mix to a soft, but not sticky dough with the milk. Turn out on to a lightly floured board, knead quickly till smooth then roll out to about half an inch in thickness. Cut into rounds with a small cutter and arrange them, close together, on top of the **hot** Goulash. Brush tops with milk and bake towards the top of a hot oven 10 to 15 minutes. Serve piping hot with hot vegetables.

PICKLED BRISKET OF BEEF

6lb salted brisket of beef; 3 slices of bacon; 2 carrots; 1 onion; bunch of savoury herbs; salt and pepper; cloves, all-spice, mace.

Put the beef in a stew-jar together with the rest of the ingredients, and cover all with water. Stew gently in oven for four hours. When cooked, leave to cool, then remove from the liquid and press between two plates, under a weight.

HORSERADISH DUMPLINGS WITH BEEF CASSEROLE

Dumplings can make inexpensive casseroles of meat very special. Each time you serve them they can be different. Try fresh or dried herbs, chopped bacon, orange rind—or horseradish. Here's a recipe that will satisfy hearty family appetites.

1½lb chuck steak; 1oz dripping; 2 medium onions, finely sliced; 1 can tomato puree (2¼oz size); pinch mixed herbs; 1oz flour, well seasoned with salt and pepper; 1 pint water; 1 stick celery, sliced.

Horseradish Dumplings:

4oz self-raising flour; 1½oz shredded suet; 3 to 4 tablespoons cold water; 1 teaspoon salt; 1 tablespoon horseradish sauce.

Cut meat into pieces and toss in well seasoned flour. Melt dripping in a large frying pan or saucepan and gently fry onion until golden. Add the meat and fry for a further 5 minutes, turning until meat is brown. Remove from heat and blend in water and tomato puree. Add celery and herbs. Return to heat and bring to boil. Turn mixture into a 3 pint casserole. Cover with lid and cook in the middle of a moderate oven for 2 hours.

Dumplings: Sift together flour and salt, then add suet. Blend horseradish sauce and water together. Add to flour and mix to a soft dough. Shape into 8 small balls and cook, covered, in casserole for last 45 minutes of cooking time.

YORKSHIRE BEEF MOULD

Cut **1lb shin beef** into small pieces and put through mincer (raw). Do the same with **4oz lean ham (raw).** Add a **very small pinch of salt and a small teacup of fine breadcrumbs** and mix together with a **tablespoon of boiling water.** Lastly add **1 well-beaten egg.** Mix to smooth consistency and press into a basin. Tie a butter paper over and then a cloth and tie well down. Steam for exactly three hours. Take into pantry just as it is and leave overnight. Then remove covers and tip out. It will be lovely and firm and of a delicious flavour.

SPICED MUTTON

Bone the **joint of mutton,** rub it well with **pepper (black pepper is best), a little powdered thyme, a pinch of mace and fine oatmeal** mixed together. Cover thickly with mutton dripping and wrap the whole in cabbage leaves. Roast very slowly, allowing at least twenty minutes for each pound of meat. Baste well two or three times during the cooking, and to make it something really special add cupful of cider to the fat in the roasting tin.

STUFFED BREAST OF VEAL

1 3lb boned breast of veal; salt and pepper; ½ oz lard
Stuffing:
1 green pepper; 4oz calf's liver, finely chopped; 1 small onion, finely chopped; ½ oz butter; ¾lb sausage meat; 8oz fresh white breadcrumbs; 1 teaspoon mixed dried herbs; 1 level tablespoon chopped parsley; ½ level teaspoon salt; pinch pepper; 1 egg.

Remove seeds from pepper. Blanch by covering with boiling water for 1 minute and cut into small squares. Lightly fry chopped liver and onion in butter for two to three minutes. Mix together sausage meat, breadcrumbs and blend with chopped liver and onion mixture. Add herbs and seasoning and bind with beaten egg. Place meat on a board, flatten to an oblong shape and spread with stuffing. Roll up tightly and tie neatly with string at ¾ in. intervals. Sprinkle liberally with seasoned flour. Place in roasting tin with lard and baste frequently during roasting. Bake in a moderately hot oven for 2 hours.

As an alternative to basting, spread joint with lard, season and wrap in foil. Bake as above. Remove foil after 2¼ hours and bake for further 20 minutes until joint is well browned.

For a small joint adjust the quantity of stuffing accordingly.

JUGGED HARE

1 hare; 1lb stewing steak; 1 large onion stuck with 3 or 4 cloves; 1 teaspoon mixed herbs; a small piece of lemon rind; stock or water sufficient to cover the hare; butter; flour; seasoning.

Skin, clean and wipe the hare very thoroughly. Joint it, dip the pieces in seasoned flour and fry in the butter till well browned. Place in a large casserole or pan, together with the onion, herbs and lemon rind, add the stewing steak cut into small pieces, and seasoning to taste. Cover with the stock or water. Cook gently in a moderate oven for about three hours. Make sure the lid fits well; this helps to retain all the flavour in the casserole. To make it something special, a couple of glasses of port wine may be added.

SAGE COBBLER OF LAMB

2lb lamb (meat from shoulder, neck or breast); 1oz well-seasoned flour; 1oz cooking fat, lard or dripping; 2 medium onions, peeled and thinly-sliced; about 1½ breakfast cups of chopped celery or turnips; 1 pint water; 2 level tablespoons tomato puree; ¼ teaspoon salt.

Divide meat into one inch pieces and coat with seasoned flour. Melt fat in a pan, add vegetables and fry over medium heat till light gold. Move to one side and fry meat. Transfer to a two to three pint casserole dish then pour over water mixed with the tomato puree and salt. Cover with lid and cook in the centre of the oven at 335°F. or gas Mark 3 for two hours.

Topping:

8oz plain flour; 2 rounded teaspoons baking powder; 1 level teaspoon salt; 2oz butter or margarine; ½ teaspoon sage; 6 tablespoons milk (or 1 egg and 2 tablespoons milk).

Sift flour, baking powder and salt. Rub in fat, add sage, then mix to a soft, but not sticky, dough with milk. Turn out on to lightly-floured board and knead quickly. Roll into a round, half an inch in thickness. Cut into six equal-sized triangles with sharp knife. Remove casserole from oven, uncover, then arrange the scone triangles on top of meat. Brush with milk, return casserole to oven and bake at 425°F. or gas Mark 7 for twenty minutes.

LAMB PIE

1½lb middle neck lamb or mutton; ½ level teaspoon ground mace or nutmeg; about 1 pint of water; pepper and salt.

Sauce:

¼ pint of stock from lamb; ¼ pint milk; 1oz butter; 1oz flour; 2oz button mushrooms.

Pastry:

4oz plain flour; 4oz self-raising flour; pinch salt; 4oz lard; 2 to 3 tablespoons water.

Ask the butcher to divide the meat into small portions. Put lamb, pepper, salt, mace or nutmeg in a pan. Press meat down and cover with water. Simmer over a low heat until tender (about 1 to 1½ hours). Remove meat from the bone and cut into 1in. pieces, removing excess fat. Skim fat off liquid and strain.

Wash and drain mushrooms. Slice and fry gently in butter. Add flour and cook for a few moments. Remove from the heat and slowly blend in stock and milk. Return to the heat, bring to the boil, stirring all the time until the liquid thickens. Turn into a bowl and add meat. Allow to cool.

Sieve together flour and salt. Lightly rub fat into flour until mixture resembles fine breadcrumbs. Add water and mix to a dough. Lightly knead until smooth. Divide pastry into two. On a floured board roll into two large circles to fit an 8 to 9 inch deep ovenproof plate. Lift the first circle on to the plate. Pile lamb mixture in the centre and moisten edges of pastry. Put second circle on top. Gently press edges of pastry to seal and trim the edges. Carefully make a cross in the centre of the pastry and pull back flaps. Decorate edge of pastry with a fork. Glaze with milk and bake in a hot oven for 30 minutes until golden brown.

LAMB, POTATO KEBABS

12 cubes lean raw lamb (approximately 1 inch square and ½-inch

thick); **12 small or quartered potatoes; 2 sheeps' kidneys; 1½-2oz butter; pepper and salt; 1 sliced onion; 2 tablespoons cooking oil.**

Skin the kidneys, cut into small pieces and remove cores. Sprinkle lamb and kidneys with pepper, salt, sliced onion and oil. Leave for 1-2 hours turning meat occasionally. Place potatoes in cold salted water and bring to the boil, drain well. Thread lamb, kidneys and potatoes alternately on 4 long skewers, baste well with melted butter. Lay Kebabs across a roasting tin and bake in a hot oven for 25 minutes. Baste continually with the melted butter. Serve with tomato sauce.

PORK HEDGEHOG
½lb belly port; 1 onion; ½lb stale breadcrumbs; 1 teaspoon sage; 2oz dripping; some stale crusts of bread; 1lb cooking apples; 1oz margarine; salt and pepper.

Mince the pork and onion and mix with breadcrumbs, sage and seasoning, mould into an oval shape and place in a baking tin with the dripping. Stick fingers of stale bread all over (like the bristles of a hedgehog) and bake in a moderate oven for one hour, basting during the time. When done pour off the dripping, peel and core the apples, cut into thick slices and fry slowly in a frying pan for about ten minutes. Arrange round the hedgehog and serve.

BAKED PORK CHOPS WITH DRESSING
4 pork chops; 6 slices of stale bread (milk or water to moisten); 1 finely minced onion; (I grated mine) ½ teaspoon salt; ½ teaspoon pepper; ½ teaspoon sage; 1 egg, well beaten.

Pan fry the chops until golden brown, cover with water and simmer gently for twenty-five minutes. Meanwhile, add enough milk or water to the bread to just moisten it. When soft, press out any excess liquid and pour off, then add the onion, seasoning, sage and beaten egg. Put the pork chops into a baking dish, cover with the dressing and bake in a moderate oven about one and a half hours, basting the dressing frequently with the liquor in which the chops were simmered.

PORK PUDDING
1½lb flour; ¾lb raisins; a little salt; 1lb salt pork; 1 egg.

Chop up the pork, but not too finely, and mix with the flour and salt, then add the raisins previously stoned and mix to a stiff batter with eggs and milk. Put into a greased baking tin and bake until well cooked.

HASLET
1½lb lean pork (minced); 4oz bread; sage, pepper, salt.

Soak 4oz bread and squeeze as dry as possible, add a little fine sage and pepper and salt to taste. Mix with the minced pork and form into shape, wrap in a piece of foil, put on a tin and bake in a moderate oven one hour. One lady suggests adding a minced onion. Mostly eaten cold.

YORKSHIREMAN'S GOOSE
½lb of beef liver; 1 onion; 1lb potatoes, 1 teaspoon flour; ½ teaspoon of pounded sage; salt and pepper.

Wash, wipe and slice liver. Put the flour on a plate, season liver with salt and pepper and dip it in the flour. Place the slices in layers in a greased dish. Parboil the onion, mince it, mix it with the sage, and sprinkle between the layers of liver, pouring in sufficient stock (or water) to come half way up the dish. Parboil the potatoes, cut them in slices, place them over the top of liver to form a crust, and bake for an hour until the top potatoes are nicely browned.

LIVER AND BACON HOT-POT

1lb pig's liver; ½lb streaky bacon; apples; onions; breadcrumbs; salt and pepper; chopped parsley and marjoram

Chop the apples and onions, cut bacon into very thin slices and liver into thin pieces. Place a layer of liver in a greased casserole or pie dish, cover with bacon, sprinkle with breadcrumbs, parsley, onions, marjoram, salt and pepper. Add one thick layer of chopped cooking apples. Repeat these layers until dish is full, the last layer being breadcrumbs; fill dish right up with lukewarm water. Bake in a moderately hot oven for two hours, covering the dish. Add a little more water if it gets too dry. Half an hour before the cooking is finished, remove the cover to brown top. Serve very hot.

STUFFED LIVER

1lb of liver in one piece; slices of fat bacon; forcemeat stuffing.

Par-boil the liver, allow to cool, slice lengthwise into two pieces, spread one piece with forcemeat and place the other piece on top. Tie firmly together and cover with the bacon. Put in a greased casserole, cover with baking foil and cook in a moderately hot oven until tender about 1½ hours. Remove the bacon and keep for garnishing. Pour over the liver a thick onion gravy made with the liquid left after par-boiling the liver.

HUNTER'S ROLL

8oz self-raising flour; 1 level teaspoon salt; 4oz suet, finely chopped; ¼ pint water; 4oz bacon; 6oz liver; 1 level tablespoon chopped parsley.

Sift together flour and salt. Add suet. Mix to a soft, but not sticky dough, with water. Knead lightly on a floured board, till smooth. Roll out into an oblong approximately 10in. x 12in. Finely chop bacon and liver. Mix with parsley and spread to within half an

inch of the edges of pastry. Moisten edges with water, then roll up loosely, as for a Swiss roll. Wrap well in greased, greaseproof paper and steam over boiling water for 2 hours. Serve on a heated plate with gravy and vegetables.

HEART AND KIDNEY PUDDING

Crust: ½lb self-raising flour; salt; ¼lb suet; cold water.

Filling: 1 pig's heart; 2 pig's kidneys; 1 tablespoon flour; salt and pepper; water.

Mix together flour, suet and salt and make into a soft dough with cold water. Roll out and line a basin with part of the dough, leaving enough for a lid. Cut heart and kidneys into small pieces, after removing skin, roll in seasoned flour and add sufficient water to cover. Place in lined basin, cover with remains of pastry for a lid and steam for three hours.

DEVILLED SAUSAGES AND KIDNEYS

1lb beef sausages; 3oz margarine; 3 tablespoons breadcrumbs; 1½ teaspoons curry powder; 1½ teaspoons brown sauce.

Seasoning, kidneys, tomatoes and mashed potatoes for serving and garnishing.

Boil sausages steadily for ten minutes. Skin and halve. Cream margarine, add curry, crumbs, sauce and seasoning. This mixture is then spread on cut sides of sausages and grilled. Then arrange around a pyramid of mashed potatoes with grilled half kidneys on top. Tomatoes grilled for garnishing.

YORKSHIRE TOAD

1½lb boiled potatoes; 2 large sliced onions; 1lb pork sausages; salt and pepper.

Batter: 4oz plain flour; 1 large egg; ½ pint milk; salt.

Slice the potatoes ¼in. thick. Place in a baking tin with the sausages and onions, and put into a hot oven.

Sieve together the flour and salt into a basin. Add the egg and some of the milk. Beat well for about 5 minutes. Leave to stand.

When the potato mixture has been in the oven for about 20 minutes, add the rest of the milk to the batter, stir well and pour over the top. Return to the oven for 30 minutes until well risen, crisp and brown.

Fish Dishes

POTATO SEA BAKE

1lb potatoes; ¼lb mushrooms; ½lb tomatoes; (skinned and mashed up) 1lb fresh filleted haddock or cod; 1oz butter; salt and pepper.

Remove skin from fish and then place fish in a lightly greased pie-dish, cover and bake in a moderately hot oven for about 20 minutes until cooked. Meanwhile saute the mushrooms in the butter and boil the potatoes in salted water. When potatoes are just cooked, drain and cut into slices about ¼in. thick. Remove fish from the oven, cover with the mushrooms, sliced potatoes and tomatoes. Return to the oven and allow to heat through. Garnish with parsley.

FISH MAYONNAISE (pack in cartons for picnics)

1lb fish cooked; 1oz flour; 1 level teaspoon mustard; 1 level teaspoon salt; 3 to 4 tablespoons vinegar (preferably white); 4 tomatoes; 1oz margarine; ½ pint milk; 2 level teaspoons sugar; ¼ level teaspoon pepper; lettuce leaves; ½ pint peas, fresh cooked; a little chopped cucumber.

Make a sauce with the margarine, flour and milk. Add mustard, sugar, salt and pepper to the vinegar and mix well. Pour into the sauce, mix well. Allow to cool. Arrange the flaked fish on a bed of lettuce leaves, border with peas and tomatoes. Pour the sauce over the fish to cover it and sprinkle with the chopped cucumber.

COD SPECIAL

4 thin slices middle cod; tablespoon finely chopped parsley dessertspoon lemon juice; 2½oz butter or margarine; salt; cayenne pepper.

Wash the fish and drain it. Butter a fireproof dish, put in the slices of fish, just overlapping one another. Beat the butter to a very soft cream and work into it the parsley and seasoning, adding the lemon juice very gradually. Spread this mixture over the fish, cover with buttered paper and bake for 10 to 15 minutes in a moderately hot oven. Serve in the dish in which it was cooked.

HADDOCK SCRAMBLE

1lb smoked haddock fillets; 3 eggs; 2 tablespoonsful milk; pepper to taste; 1oz butter; triangles of toast; tomatoes.

Poach the haddock in a little water for 7 minutes, drain, skin and flake. Whisk the eggs with the milk and pepper. Melt the butter in a thick pan and scramble the eggs lightly; just before the eggs are cooked, fold in the flaked fish. Turn the egg mixture on to a warmed serving dish, garnish with triangles of toast and halved tomatoes. Serve at once.

FINNAN SOUFFLE

1½lb finnan haddock; 1oz margarine; 1oz flour; ¼ pint milk; 1 teaspoonful lemon juice; 3 eggs.

Grease a 7½in. souffle dish. Cover the fish with boiling water and leave to stand for 2 minutes, then remove the skin and bones and flake the fish. Melt the fat in a saucepan, add the flour and cook for 2-3 minutes then gradually stir in the milk; bring to the boil and cook, stirring, for 2 minutes. Set aside to cool. Add the lemon juice to the cooled mixture, stir in the egg yolks one at a time, then stir in the flaked fish. Beat the egg whites until stiff, then lightly fold into the fish mixture. Pour into the prepared souffle dish and bake in a moderate oven for 35-40 minutes. Serve at once.

CRUNCHY-TOPPED HADDOCK CASSEROLE

1lb fresh skinned fillet of haddock; 2oz button mushrooms, sliced; 1 tablespoon chopped parsley; salt and pepper; 1 large onion, chopped; 1oz butter; 8oz fresh tomatoes, skinned and sliced.

Topping: 6 slices crustless bread, well buttered; 1oz grated Cheddar cheese.

Arrange haddock fillets in a buttered shallow ovenproof dish. Fry onion in butter until soft, add mushrooms and fry for a further minute. Stir in tomatoes and parsley, season well with salt and pepper. Pour over fish. Cover and bake in a moderate oven, for about 40 minutes.

For Topping: Cut slices of bread into triangles then arrange on a baking sheet close together. Sprinkle over grated cheese and bake in oven on shelf below fish. Arrange triangles round the outside of dish before serving.

STUFFED BAKED HERRINGS

4 herrings; tomato chutney; ½oz butter or margarine; juice of 1 lemon; salt and pepper.

Clean, split and bone the herrings. Spread each one with tomato chutney and fold together. Butter thickly a suitable oven dish and arrange the herrings in it. Season with salt and pepper and sprinkle with lemon juice. Cover with greaseproof paper and cook for fifteen minutes in a moderate oven. Remove the paper for the last five minutes. A pleasant contrast is to serve these with tomato salad, dressed in oil and vinegar or chopped parsley or chive.

POTATO KIPPER SCRAMBLE

1½lb new potatoes; 6 eggs; seasoning; 1 or 2 kippers, grilled; 2oz butter; 1 tablespoon cream or top of milk.

Scrub new potatoes, cover with boiling salted water. Cook for 15 to 20 minutes. Carefully remove kipper from bones and flake, keep warm. Beat eggs, salt and pepper lightly together. Melt butter in a thick saucepan, pour in eggs, keeping heat low, stir all the time. Remove from heat, stir in cream and most of the kipper. Drain potatoes, arrange in ring, pile eggs in centre and decorate with remaining kipper.

PLAICE ARLINGTON

8 fillets of plaice, skinned; 3oz streaky bacon, chopped; 5 x ¼in. thick slices white bread, from a large loaf crumbled; 1 egg, beaten; salt and pepper; 1 small onion, finely chopped; 1 level teaspoon mixed herbs; rind and juice of ½ lemon; 2oz butter.

Sauce: 1oz butter; ½ pint milk; juice of ½ lemon; ½ pint prawns; 1oz flour; salt and pepper; 1 egg yolk.

Season fillets and roll up, skin side inside, leaving a hole in the centre of each. Arrange in a greased shallow baking dish. Fry bacon and onions gently together until cooked. Remove from heat and stir in crumbs, herbs, lemon rind, lemon juice and egg. Season to taste. Spoon mixture into centre of each fillet. Dot with butter and cover with foil. Bake in a moderate oven for 15 minutes.

To Make Sauce: Melt butter in a saucepan, stir in flour and cook for 1 minute. Gradually add milk and bring to the boil stirring constantly. Remove from heat and add seasoning and lemon juice and then beat in egg yolk. Add prawns, reserving 8 for garnishing.

Pour off liquor from fish and blend into the sauce. Garnish fish with prawns and serve sauce separately.

SALMON LAYER BETTY

Crumb Mixture: 6oz white breadcrumbs; 3oz butter; salt and pepper.

Salmon Filling: 1 x 7¾ oz canned salmon; 1oz butter; 1oz flour; ½ pint milk; juice of half a lemon; 1 egg yolk; ¼ cucumber (peeled and cut in ¼ cubes); salt and pepper; 1 heaped teaspoon chopped parsley.

Fry breadcrumbs gently in butter until golden brown. Season lightly with salt and pepper.

Drain and flake salmon. Melt butter in a pan, add flour and cook for a few minutes without browning. Remove from the heat and add the milk gradually. Return to the heat. Bring to the boil and allow to thicken, stirring continuously. Add lemon juice, then remove from the heat and stir in egg yolk. Add salmon. Heat for a further 2 minutes without boiling. Add cucumber and season with salt and pepper. Arrange layers of salmon and breadcrumbs in a 1½ pint heated dish, finishing with a layer of breadcrumbs. Bake in a fairly hot oven for 15 minutes. Sprinkle with parsley and serve.

SALMON CROQUETTES

1oz butter; 1oz flour; ¼ pint milk; egg and breadcrumbs; 6oz cold cooked salmon, fresh or tinned; seasoning.

Melt the butter and stir in the flour. Add the milk and stir until the mixture leaves the sides of the pan. Add the seasoning and the flaked fish. Turn on to a wet plate and when cold divide into equal parts and make into croquettes. Fry in deep fat, after coating in egg and breadcrumbs. Serve with parsley and lemon.

A Special Selection

The mouth-watering selection of recipes illustrated on the following eight pages are described below and on pages 45 - 47. They represent a personal choice from the hundreds that have been sent in by Dalesman readers over the years.

BAKED STUFFED MACKEREL WITH CIDER SAUCE   Fig. 1

Stuffing:

½oz butter or margarine; 1 small onion, grated; 2 sticks celery, finely chopped; 2 medium cooking apples, peeled, cored and finely chopped; 4oz white breadcrumbs; 2 level tablespoons chopped parsley; 1 egg, beaten; salt and pepper.

4 large or 6 small mackerel, heads removed, cleaned and boned; ¼ pint dry cider; 1 medium cooking apple, peeled, cored and thinly sliced.

Sauce:

¼ pint dry cider; 1 tablespoon lemon juice; 2 level teaspoons cornflour; salt and pepper; 3 tablespoons single cream or top of milk.

Lemon wedges and parsley for garnish.

Melt butter or margarine in pan and gently fry onion and celery for 5 minutes. Add apple and cook gently for a further 4 minutes, stirring occasionally. Remove from heat and stir in breadcrumbs, parsley and beaten egg. Season to taste.

Divide stuffing between mackerel and spread over inside of each fish. Fold mackerel over to enclose stuffing and place in a shallow greased ovenproof dish. Cut apple slices in half and arrange over mackerel. Pour over cider, cover with a lid or foil, and bake at 325°F., Gas Mark 3, for 35 minutes.

Remove fish and apple from ovenproof dish and place on a serving plate. Keep warm. For the sauce, strain liquor from the dish and mix with cider. Place in a pan. Blend lemon juice and cornflour and stir into pan. Bring to boil, stirring continuously and boil for 1 minute. Season and stir in cream or top of milk. Serve mackerel garnished with lemon wedges and parsley, and hand sauce separately.

Serves 4 or 6.

1. BAKED STUFFED
MACKEREL

2. EASTER FISH PIE

3. STUFFED
MARROW RINGS

4 (left). DUMPLING
TOPPERS

5 (right). TAFFETY
TARTS

6 (left). PICNIC BURGERS
7 (right). CURATE'S EYE

8. KEBAB ROLLS
TUNA AND
CUCUMBER
ROLLS

EASTER FISH PIE
Fig. 2

½ pint milk; 1 onion; 1 clove garlic (optional); salt; pepper; 2oz butter; 1oz flour; 1 x 7oz tin tuna.

Quick Flaky Pastry:
8oz plain flour; ½ level teaspoon salt; 3oz lard; 3oz hard margarine; ¼ pint water.

Put milk in a pan with chopped onion, garlic (if liked), salt and pepper. Slowly bring to the boil, remove from the heat and leave for about 20 minutes. Strain. Melt butter in a pan. Add flour and cook for a few minutes, without browning. Remove from heat and add milk gradually. Return to heat and allow to thicken. Remove from heat, and add drained, flaked tuna. Cool.

Pastry: Sieve flour and salt into a basin. Cut fat up roughly into small pieces, about ½in. cubes, with two round bladed knives one in each hand using a scissor action. Mix to a soft dough with water. Roll out on a floured board to an oblong approx. 5in. x 12in. Fold in three. Roll and fold twice more in the same way keeping folded edge always on the right. Chill between rollings if necessary. Roll out two oblongs 12in. x 8in. Place one on a baking sheet and place filling on top spreading within an inch of the sides. Damp edges. Fold second oblong in half and make slashes at ¾in. intervals ½in. from the edge, then place on top of the first oblong. Press edges together. Knock up the edges using the back of a knife. Bake in a fairly hot oven 400°F. or Gas Mark 6 for 40 minutes. Serves 4 to 6.

STUFFED MARROW RINGS
Fig. 3

1 large marrow, peeled.
Stuffing:
6 large slices white bread, crusts removed, broken into pieces; ¼ pint milk; 1 tablespoon oil; 1 onion, chopped; 8oz pig's liver, chopped; 4oz streaky bacon, rind removed, chopped; ¼ level teaspoon dried mixed herbs; salt and pepper.

Tomato Sauce:
1 tablespoon oil; 1 onion, finely chopped; 2 sticks celery, finely chopped; 2 rashers streaky bacon, rind removed, chopped; 1 (14oz) can peeled tomatoes; ¼ level teaspoon dried mixed herbs; ¼ level teaspoon sugar; salt and pepper.

Cut marrow into 4 slices, each at least 3in thick and remove seeds and pith from each slice. Place in a large pan of boiling salted water, cover and simmer for 10 minutes. Drain well and place slices in a large greased ovenproof dish.

For the stuffing, soak bread in milk and leave to stand for ½ hour. Beat well with a fork. Heat oil in a pan and fry onion gently for 5 minutes. Add liver, bacon and mixed herbs and fry for a further 5 minutes. Add to soaked bread and mix well. Season and spoon the mixture into centres of marrow slices. Bake at 375°F, Gas Mark 5, for 25-30 minutes.

For the sauce, heat oil in a pan and fry onion, celery and bacon gently for 5 minutes. Stir in tomatoes and herbs, bring to the boil, cover, and simmer for 10 minutes. Reduce to a purée. Add sugar, season well and reheat. Serve sauce separately.

DUMPLING TOPPERS
Fig. 4

These recipes are useful to keep as a reference for any time when casseroles are on the menu—and especially so when vegetables are expensive and scarce:

4oz self-raising flour; 1 level teaspoon grated lemon rind; 2oz finely shredded suet (or 1oz butter); about 3 tablespoons cold water and squeeze of lemon juice.

Mix ingredients to a firm dough. Roll into 6 or 8 small balls. Place on top of nearly cooked meat and vegetables (do not submerge in liquid) in casserole. Cover and cook about 30 minutes in a moderately hot oven.

Bacon Dumplings: Sift ½ level teaspoon dry mustard and sprinkling pepper with flour and add 1 tablespoon chopped cooked bacon or ham to above.

Spiced Apple Dumplings: Add 2 heaped tablespoons finely chopped apple, 1 tablespoon chopped onion and a grating of nutmeg. Especially good with casserole of liver or pork.

TAFFETY TARTS   Fig. 5

Pastry:

8oz plain flour; pinch of salt; 4oz butter; 2 - 3 tablespoons water.
Filling:

1lb cooking apples; 4oz soft brown sugar; 2oz sultanas; ½ level teaspoon cinnamon; ¼ teaspoon mixed spice; rind of half a lemon, grated.

To Make the Pastry:

Sieve together flour and salt. Rub in fat until mixture resembles fine breadcrumbs. Add water and mix ingredients together to a firm dough.

To Make the Filling:

Peel, core and thinly slice apples. Put a few slices to one side for topping tarts. Mix the remainder with sugar, sultanas and lemon rind and spices. Roll out pastry and cut 9 four inch circles to line greased tins. Flute edges. Fill with apple mixture and top with apple slices.

Bake in a hot oven, 400°F. or Gas Mark 6, for 30 minutes until the pastry is evenly browned and the apple tender. Leave in tins for a few moments, then lift out and cool on a wire rack. If liked brush the top with a little sieved apricot jam. Serve with cream. Makes 9 tarts.

PICNIC-BURGERS   Fig. 6

1½lb minced beef; 1 finely chopped onion; ½ cup white bread-crumbs; 1 teaspoon salt; 1 dessertspoon made mustard; 1 beaten egg; dried breadcrumbs for coating.

Mix ingredients together, binding with the beaten egg. Shape into 12 patties. Coat with breadcrumbs and lightly fry in butter, about 3 minutes each side. Serve the hamburgers in split soft rolls or baps with lightly fried onion rings.

A slice of cheese may also be added for extra flavour and nourishment.

CURATE'S EYE   Fig. 7

4 slices bread, cut ½in thick; 2½oz butter; 4 tomatoes, halved; 2oz butter; 4 eggs.

Cut out the centre of each slice of bread with a 2in plain cutter. Butter all pieces of bread on both sides. Fry 2in rounds of bread quickly until crisp and brown on both sides, together with tomatoes. Remove and keep warm. Fry one side of bread slices until crisp and brown. Turn over, reduce heat and add extra butter. Carefully drop an egg into the centre of each slice. Spoon butter over eggs continuously until cooked, about 3 minutes. Serve immediately with rounds of bread topped with tomato halves.

*

Meals out-of-doors are great fun but, with our changeable climate, it is rather chancy to make plans too far ahead. Here are some picnic ideas which can be made on the spur of the moment from a selection of rolls, and food from the storecupboard. They are certain to appeal to healthy appetites, too:-

KEBAB ROLLS

8 bridge rolls or crisp long rolls; 2oz butter; 1 tablespoon prepared mustard; 8 rashers streaky bacon; 1 x 8oz can cocktail frankfurters; 8 button mushrooms; 8 small gherkins; 8 cocktail onions.

Cut rolls lengthways to within ½ inch of side so that top is not completely detached. Spread inside with butter and then with mustard.

Cut each rasher of bacon in half, flatten with back of a knife and roll up. Dividing ingredients equally, thread bacon rolls, frankfurters, mushrooms, gherkins and onions onto 8 short metal skewers. Pieces of kidney can also be added, if available. Brush with a little oil and grill for 5-10 minutes, turning once. Place a skewer in each roll and holding roll firmly, remove skewer so that kebab food is left in roll.

Makes 8.

TUNA AND CUCUMBER ROLLS
Fig. 8

4 crisp round rolls; 1oz softened butter; 1 x 7oz can tuna, drained; 3 tablespoons thick mayonnaise; 1 tablespoon chopped chives; salt and pepper; 16 thin slices of cucumber.

Cut tops off rolls and scoop out centres. Spread insides with butter. Crumble bread from centre of rolls into a bowl, add tuna, mayonnaise, chives and seasoning, and mix well together with a fork. Line inside of rolls with cucumber slices and fill with tuna mixture. Replace lid.

Makes 4.

Sauces and Stuffings

MAYONNAISE

Put the **yolks of 2 eggs** into a basin. Add a **good pinch of salt, pepper and dry mustard.** Beat in **2 gills salad oil.** This must be done very carefully, drop by drop, beating all the time until the mixture is thick and creamy. If the oil is added too quickly the mixture will curdle.

Finally beat in **2 dessertspoons lemon juice.**

This mayonnaise will last up to a week if kept in a refrigerator or in a cool place.

LEMON SAUCE

juice 1 lemon; rind ½ lemon; 1 small teaspoonful cornflour; ½ pint water; 2oz granulated sugar.

Wash and wipe a lemon, shred rind on a grater. Add to the water and bring to the boil, add the sugar and the thickening cornflour which has been mixed with the lemon juice to a smooth paste. Stir over the fire until the sauce boils, cook for a few minutes, still stirring and serve in a hot sauceboat.

FLUFFY BRANDY SAUCE

1 egg separated; ¼ pint whipped double cream; 4oz icing sugar; 3 tablespoons brandy.

Beat the egg white until it is foamy. Add 2oz of the icing sugar, a little at a time, beating well after each addition until the mixture is stiff enough to stand up in peaks. In a second bowl, beat the egg yolk and remaining 2oz sugar until the mixture thickens. Fold into the egg white and sugar mixture together with the whipped cream and brandy.

This sauce can be made in advance and kept in the refrigerator until it is needed.

SPICED APPLE SAUCE

1lb cooking apples; 2 tablespoons water; 1/8 teaspoon grated nutmeg; 4oz granulated sugar; ¼ teaspoon cinnamon.

Wash, core and peel apples. Cut into quarters, and place in a medium sized saucepan with granulated sugar, water, cinnamon and nutmeg. Simmer gently for 20 to 25 minutes, stirring occasionally. Serve hot with the Christmas Pudding.

TOMATO SAUCE (Not for Storing)

4oz tomato puree; approx. ¼ pint stock or water; ½ teaspoon Worcester sauce; salt and pepper.

Heat ingredients together with seasoning to taste.

FRENCH DRESSING

1 tablespoon vinegar; 2 tablespoons olive oil; salt and pepper to taste; ½ teaspoon made mustard; 1 teaspoon chopped onion; 1 tablespoon chopped mint and parsley; yolk of one softly boiled egg.

Beat all together and use at once.

VINAIGRETTE SAUCE

¼ pint olive or salad oil; 2 teaspoons each of finely chopped gherkins, shallot, and parsley; 4 tablespoons vinegar; salt and pepper; 1 teaspoon made mustard.

Mix all the ingredients together and mix again before using.

FORCEMEAT STUFFING

8oz sausage meat; 1 egg; chopped parsley; mixed herbs.

Mix all ingredients thoroughly, if desired the giblets finely chopped may be added.

FORCEMEAT STUFFING (2)

2oz breadcrumbs; 1oz shredded suet; 1 teaspoon mixed herbs; 2 heaped teaspoons finely chopped parsley; milk to bind.

Mix all ingredients well together and bind with milk.

CHESTNUT STUFFING

½lb shelled chestnuts; 1 egg; 1 heaped teaspoon chopped parsley; 2oz breadcrumbs; 1 dessertspoon lemon juice.

Put chestnuts into boiling water and simmer until soft. Drain and rub through a sieve. Mix well with the rest of the ingredients.

SAGE AND ONION STUFFING

1 large onion; 1½oz fresh breadcrumbs; a good ½ teaspoon rubbed sage; salt and pepper to taste.

Peel and slice onion and cover with water. Add salt to taste and simmer until tender. Chop onion finely and add to the other ingredients using the water in which the onion cooked to moisten.

Salads

CRUNCHY GREEN SALAD

2 green apples; 2 sticks celery; 4 tablespoons mayonnaise; ½ bunch watercress; 1 tablespoon lemon juice; ¼ cucumber, peeled; 1 lettuce.

Slice unpeeled apples very thinly, toss in lemon juice. Chop celery and dice cucumber. Mix together with mayonnaise. Arrange lettuce and watercress in a bowl and pile apple mixture in the middle.

BASIC POTATO SALAD

1½lb potatoes; ¼ pint mayonnaise or vinaigrette sauce; 1 tablespoon finely chopped onion; 1 tablespoon chopped mint, parsley or other green herbs.

Boil the potatoes in their jackets. Peel and slice or dice. Add the chopped onion. Mix with enough salad dressing to moisten. If dressed while hot the potatoes soak up more dressing. Some people prefer a salad dressing while hot, others when the potatoes are cold. In either case keep the salad several hours before serving to allow the flavours to mix. Sprinkle with the chopped herbs just before serving. Instead of using onion, the bowl may be rubbed with a cut clove or garlic before putting in the potatoes.

Variations

For variety any of the following may be mixed with the potatoes:

Equal quantities of any of these vegetables: chopped cucumber; diced cooked beetroot; cooked peas; diced cooked kohl rabi; cook cauliflower; small cooked sprouts or shredded raw sprouts; shredde raw cabbage; chopped celery; cooked diced French beans; diced ra apples; flaked tunny fish or other cooked fish.

TANGY POTATO SALAD

1lb boiled diced potatoes.

Dressing: 3 tablespoons vegetable, corn nut or olive oil; salt an pepper; 1 tablespoon vinegar; pinch of sugar to taste; squeeze garlic if liked.

Blend all the dressing ingredients together in a basin. Add th potatoes, and enough relish or chutney to taste.

BEETROOT SALAD CUPS

4 medium-sized cooked beetroots; heart of a young cabba teaspoon sugar; salt; salad dressing; ½lb mixed cooked vegetabl few drops lemon juice.

Choose beetroots of a good shape and as near the same size possible. Scoop out the inside, after cutting off the top to ma them stand firm, and sprinkle each inside with the sugar, salt a lemon juice. Stand in a cold place. Chop up cooked vegetables a moisten with the dressing. Fill the cups with the mixture, and se on a bed of shredded cabbage.

CARROT AND CHEESE SALAD

½lb carrots; 4oz cheese; 1 bunch water cress; ½lb tomatoes; tablespoon finely chopped parsley; 1 tablespoon salad oil (if liked).

Clean the carrots and grate into a basin, mix with the salad oil. Grate the cheese and mix lightly into the carrots. Pile on to the centre of a dish, sprinkle the chopped parsley over the top, put watercress and halved tomatoes round the edge.

CHEESE AND CUCUMBER SALAD

4oz diced cheese; 4oz diced cucumber; ½ teaspoon lemon juice; inch each of salt, pepper and mustard; lettuce or water cress; 2 tomatoes.

Toss the diced cheese and cucumber together in the lemon juice and seasoning. Pile neatly on a bed of lettuce or watercress and garnish with tomato.

CHICORY SALAD

4 large heads prepared chicory; 2 tablespoons melted butter; tablespoon chopped parsley; small pieces of tomato; 5 hardboiled eggs; 2 tablespoons double cream; salt, pepper.

Carefully separate the remove the leaves from the chicory, stopping when you come to the central one of very small leaves. Shell the eggs, mash with a fork and mix them with the butter and cream. Season well. Fill the separated chicory leaves with the mixture, and arrange on a round serving dish with a few pieces of tomato on each. Put the cones of chicory in the middle.

DANDELION SALAD

1 handful young dandelion leaves; 2 tablespoons salad oil; salt; 1 small onion; 2 hard-boiled eggs; 1 tablespoon vinegar.

Wash and trim the dandelion leaves. Make a dressing of salt, vinegar, oil, finely chopped onion and egg. Pour this over the leaves and serve at once.

RAISIN SALAD

6oz raisins; cabbage, finely shredded (as much as required); 8oz crushed pineapple; lettuce leaves; paprika; dressing.

Rinse and drain raisins. Combine with cabbage and pineapple and half the dressing. Blend lightly. Serve on lettuce, topped with remaining dressing and garnished with paprika.

Dressing: Slowly add 2 tablespoons vinegar to 1 gill thick cream. Add 1 tablespoon castor sugar, 1 teaspoon made mustard and beat until thick.

PARTY COLESLAW

1½lb white cabbage, finely shredded; 2 red apples, cored and thinly sliced; salt and pepper; 2 carrots, coarsely grated; 2 sticks celery, chopped; generous ¼ pint home-made mayonnaise.

Mix cabbage, carrots, celery and apple together. Stir in mayonnaise. Season well.

Puddings and Sweets

APPLE CAKE

¼lb margarine or butter; ¼lb sugar; 1 egg; 8oz self-raising flour; pinch salt; milk for mixing; stewed apple.

Cream butter and sugar, add the egg, flour and salt, and enough milk to make a soft mixture. Stir well. Spread half the mixture in a greased tin (8in x 6in is a good size). Cover with rather thick sweetened stewed apples (we like it flavoured with a small piece of lemon cooked with the apple). Cover with the remainder of the batter mixture. Bake in a moderate oven till well cooked through and browned on the top (about thirty minutes).

APPLE FLIP

Prepare 1lb cooking apples and stew until soft, add the juice of half a lemon and four tablespoons of sugar. Beat up very stiffly the white of 1 egg, mix lightly into the apples. Put into a serving dish and, when cool, pour over a pint of custard and, when quite cold, decorate with whipped cream.

APPLE MERINGUE PUDDING

1lb cooking apples (cored and halved); juice and grated rind of half an orange; 3oz sugar; ¼ pint water; 6oz day-old white bread, cut into ½ inch cubes; 2oz butter; 2 egg yolks; 1 level teaspoon cinnamon.

Meringue: 2 egg whites; 3oz castor sugar.

Gently stew apples with the orange juice and rind, sugar a water. Drain fruit and reserve syrup. Pour hot syrup over bre cubes and soak seven to ten minutes. Cream butter, beat in e yolks, then mix with the soaked bread cubes, drained fruit a cinnamon. Turn into a two pint, greased heatproof dish, then ba in the centre of a moderate oven at 355°F. or gas Mark 4, thirty to thirty-five minutes or till set.

Make the meringue with the egg whites and sugar, and pile top of pudding. Return to cool oven and cook till meringue i pale gold—fifteen to twenty minutes at 310°F. or gas Mark 2.

APPLE CRACKLE PUDDING

8oz self-raising flour; pinch salt; 1 level teaspoon cinnam ½ level teaspoon nutmeg; 4oz margarine; 4oz caster sugar; cooking apples, peeled, cored and very finely sliced; 2 medium eg beaten; 6 tablespoons milk.

Sift dry ingredients into a bowl. Rub in margarine then stir sugar and apples. Mix to a thick batter with the eggs and milk stir till smooth. Turn into a well-greased 7 to 8-inch round c tin. Bake in the centre of moderate oven about 1 hour. Serve wa with custard or sweet white sauce.

SPICED APPLE CHARLOTTE

Crumb mixture: 6oz fine white breadcrumbs; 4oz chopped suet; 2oz granulated sugar.

Fruit Mixture: 1oz butter; 2 tablespoons water; 1½lb cooking apples (peeled, cored and cut into neat, small dice); 2oz brown sugar; 2oz sultanas or seedless raisins; ¼ level teaspoon cinnamon or spice.

Well grease a deep pie dish (about 2 pint size). Mix the breadcrumbs, suet and granulated sugar well together and press three quarters of it on to bottom and sides of pie dish.

Melt butter in a pan, then add water, apples and brown sugar. Cover and heat gently, shaking and stirring occasionally, till apples are well glazed but not too soft. Remove from heat and stir in sultanas and cinnamon. Pour into prepared pie dish, then top with remaining crumb mixture, pressing down neatly. Wipe edge of dish, then sprinkle crumbs with a layer of brown sugar and dot with butter. Bake in the centre of a moderate oven ¾ to 1 hour, till golden brown.

ADAM AND EVE PUDDING

1lb apples; 4oz sugar; 4oz butter; 6oz self-raising flour; 2 eggs; a little milk.

Stew the apples in a little water and sweeten to taste. Place in greased pie dish. Cream the butter and the sugar, add the eggs and the flour and mix with milk to a fairly soft consistency. Spread over the apples and bake in a moderate oven for about 30 minutes.

BLACKBERRY ROLY POLY

8oz plain flour; 1 level teaspoon baking powder; ½ level teaspoon salt; 2oz butter; 1oz castor sugar; 2 level teaspoons finely grated lemon rind; 5 to 6 tablespoons cold milk to mix.

Filling: 12oz fresh blackberries; 2 to 3oz castor sugar.

Topping: beaten egg or milk; 2 level teaspoons castor sugar; 1oz butter.

Sift flour, baking powder and salt and rub in fat finely. Stir in sugar and lemon rind. Mix to a soft dough with milk, knead lightly on a floured board till smooth, then roll out into a rectangle, approximately twelve inches by ten inches. Turn dough over, then cover with 10oz fruit to within one inch of edges. Moisten edges with water, sprinkle fruit with sugar, then roll up like a Swiss roll, starting from one of the shorter sides. Press joins well together to seal, then transfer to a heatproof dish. Make three slits in top of roll, brush with egg or milk and sprinkle with sugar. Dot small pieces of butter on the top, pour 3 tablespoons water into the dish then add remaining blackberries. Bake in the centre of a hot oven 425°F. or gas Mark 7, for fifteen minutes, then reduce to moderate, 355°F. or gas Mark 5, for twenty-five or thirty minutes. Serve hot with cream or custard.

NO-BAKE BLACKBERRY BETTY

½lb cooking apples; ½lb blackberries; 2oz sugar.

Crumb mixture: 6oz fresh white breadcrumbs (1 pint), 2oz butter, melted; 2oz soft brown sugar.

A few uncooked, ripe blackberries for decoration.

Peel each apple and cut into quarters. Remove the core and slice apple thinly.

Gently stew apples, blackberries and sugar together with one tablespoon water until fruit is tender.

Melt butter in a saucepan. Remove from heat and mix in the crumbs and sugar. Take six individual glasses or one 1-pint glass bowl. Fill with alternate layers of fruit and crumb mixture, finishing with a layer of crumb mixture. Leave to stand a few hours, preferably overnight. Decorate with raw blackberries and serve with cream.

BLACKBERRY CUSTARD

Peel, core and slice **1lb cooking apples** and cook them until soft in a pan rubbed with **butter**, adding the smallest amount of **water** if they are dry. Add **2lbs blackberries**, and continue to cook until they too are soft, then rub through a sieve and sweeten to taste while the mixture is still hot. When cold blend with **a pint of custard**, make either with **1 pint of milk and 2 level tablespoonfuls of custard powder**, or **1 pint of milk, 3 eggs and 1oz sugar.** Serve cold.

CHERRY CRUMBLE

4oz plain flour; 2oz margarine; 2oz sugar; 1lb cherries; ¼ pint water; 4oz sugar; ½oz or 1 heaped tablespoon cornflour.

Wash and stalk the cherries and put 12 of the best aside for garnish. Stew the rest of the cherries in ¼ pint water and 4ozs sugar, for 5 minutes. Divide the cherries between 4 small dishes (approximately 4in. in diameter). Thicken the juice with the cornflour blended with a little cold water. Pour on top of cherries and allow to cool.

Rub the margarine into the flour until the mixture resembles fine breadcrumbs. Mix in 2oz sugar. Sprinkle crumble mixture on top of cherries in small dishes. Bake in the middle of a fairly hot oven for 10 to 15 minutes. Garnish with cherries and serve with cream.

DATE AND ORANGE PUDDING

6oz dates (unstoned weight); 6oz plain flour; 2 rounded teaspoons baking powder; 2oz white breadcrumbs; 4oz finely chopped suet; 3oz castor sugar; grated rind of 1 orange; 2 medium eggs, beaten; approx. 4 tablespoons milk.

Well grease a pudding basin or mould and decorate base and sides with 3oz stoned dates. Chop remainder. Sift flour and baking powder into bowl, add breadcrumbs, suet, sugar, chopped dates and rind, then mix to a dropping consistency with the egg and 4 tablespoons milk, or a little more if necessary to get correct consistency. Turn mixture into prepared basin or mould, cover to with greased greaseproof paper or aluminium foil and steam steadi for two hours. Unmould on to a warm plate and serve with fres orange slices and golden orange sauce or custard.

Golden Orange Sauce: Juice of 1 large orange and 1 lemon made to ¾ pint with water, 1 rounded dessertspoon arrowroot, rounded tablespoons golden syrup, grated rind of 1 orange.

Mix arrowroot to a smooth paste with a little of the fruit jui and water. Heat remainder, add syrup, stir till dissolved then po over paste. Return to pan and cook, stirring, till sauce thickens ar becomes clear. Add rind and pour into warm sauceboat or jug.

DATE SOUFFLE

½lb stoned dates; 1 cup water; 1 tablespoon lemon juice; 4 e whites.

Cook the dates in the water until they become a mush. Add lem juice and stir in stiffly beaten egg whites. Pour into a butter dish, stand in a pan of hot water and bake until firm. Serve wi whipped cream or a pouring custard made from the egg yolks.

FIG CUSTARD

½lb figs; ½ pint milk; ¼ cup sugar; 2oz breadcrum (wholemeal); pinch nutmeg; 2 eggs.

Split figs and line a buttered casserole with them, seed side figs next to casserole. Beat the eggs, add the milk, sugar, crum and nutmeg. Pour very carefully into the casserole and bake 325°F. for about one hour. Serve either hot or cold.

FIG PIE

short crust pastry; ½lb figs; cornflour; ½ teaspoon mixed spice; dessertspoon treacle.

Put the figs into a saucepan with just enough water to cover and stew till tender. Thicken the liquid with cornflour, add spice and treacle. Mix well, put into the lined pie dish, cover with short crust pastry and bake until browned in a hot oven.

RICH ORANGE PUDDING

6oz plain flour; ½ level teaspoon mixed spice; 8oz fresh white breadcrumbs; 6oz soft brown sugar; 6oz sultanas; 1 tablespoon orange marmalade; finely grated rind of half lemon; 3 eggs, beaten; level teaspoon ginger; pinch salt; 6oz shredded suet; 6oz raisins; oz chopped candied peel; 2oz finely chopped walnuts; finely grated rind of 1 orange; ¼ pint milk.

Sift dry ingredients into bowl. Add crumbs, suet, sugar, fruit, nuts marmalade and rind then mix to a stiff consistency with the eggs and milk. Stir thoroughly till mixture is well blended then turn into a well-greased 2 to 2½ pint pudding basin. Cover securely with double thickness of well-greased greaseproof paper or aluminium foil and steam steadily for 5 hours. Serve with orange sauce.

Orange Sauce: 2oz sugar; ¼ teaspoon salt; 1 teaspoon finely grated orange rind; 1oz butter; 1 level teaspoon arrowroot; ½ pint boiling water; 1½ tablespoons orange juice; 1½ tablespoons lemon juice.

Mix together sugar, arrowroot and salt; gradually stir in hot water, bring to the boil and cook 5 minutes, stirring until smooth, thickened and clear; stir in rind, juice and butter.

BAKED PEACH PUDDING

Heat 1 pint milk until it steams then pour it over 3oz fresh

breadcrumbs. Cool for twenty minutes then stir in a **pinch of salt, 5oz sugar, a grating of nutmeg and 3 small beaten eggs.** Drain a **small tin of sliced peaches** and fold these in. Turn into a buttered casserole and bake in a moderate oven for 1¼ hours. Serve warm with pouring cream. In season **1lb pitted cherries** may be used instead of peaches.

PEACH CRUMBLE

½lb dried peaches, cooked or 1 medium sized tin of peaches; 4oz self-raising flour; 3oz margarine; 3oz soft brown sugar; 2oz porridge oats.

Rub together flour, oats, margarine and sugar until they resemble bread crumbs. Put peaches and juice into a pie dish, cover with the crumble topping. Bake in a moderate oven for 15 to 20 minutes or until golden brown on top. Delicious hot with whipped cream.

SUGAR PLUM RING

8oz self-raising flour; large pinch salt; 2oz butter; ½oz caster sugar; about ¼ pint cold milk to mix.

Coating: 2oz butter, 2oz caster sugar mixed with 1 heaped teaspoon cinnamon.

A few blanched almonds, seeded raisins and halved glace cherries, a tablespoon marmalade or honey.

Sift together flour and salt. Rub in butter, add sugar then mix to a soft, but not sticky, dough with the milk. Form quickly into 18 balls, dip in melted fat then coat all over with sugar and cinnamon. Arrange balls (with a little space between each) in two layers in a well greased 7 to 8 inch ring mould, scattering with almonds, seeded raisins and cherries in between. Bake towards the top of a moderately hot oven for 20 to 25 minutes. Remove from oven, brush top with warmed marmalade or honey and serve warm with cream.

PRUNE AND APPLE WHIP

1lb prunes; 2 good-sized eating apples, grated; 1 tablespoon brown sugar; white of 1 egg.

Cook the prunes until tender, allow to cool, remove the stones and sieve. Add the grated apples and sugar. Beat the white of egg until stiff and fold into the prunes. Top with whipped cream.

RASPBERRY PANCAKES

4oz flour; 1 egg; ½ pint milk.

Sift the flour and salt into a large bowl. Add the egg, th gradually add half the milk. Stir the flour from the sides of the bo using a wooden spoon. Beat well until the mixture is smooth. Gen stir in the rest of the milk.

With a bristle brush or piece of paper, lightly grease frying p with cooking oil or melted lard. Heat until fat is hot. Pour or wi off any surplus oil or fat. Pour 2 to 3 tablespoons batter into t pan. Quickly tilt the pan in all directions, so the batter covers t entire base of the pan. Cook until the underside of the pancake golden. Gently turn over with a broad-bladed knife, or toss. Co until this side is golden. Turn out of the pan on to greaseprc paper to cool.

Filling: 1 12oz packet frozen raspberries; ¼ pint water; 1oz sug 1 level tablespoon cornflour.

Allow raspberries to defrost. Put the juice that has drained fr the raspberries in a small pan with sugar and water, bring to boil. Blend cornflour with a little cold water in a basin, add boiling liquid from the pan, stirring continuously. Return t mixture to the pan. Bring to the boil and allow to thicken. C slightly, then add raspberries. Spread each hot pancake with portion of raspberries and sauce and fold over. Serve with fr whipped cream.

RHUBARB AND GINGER PUDDING

8oz self-raising flour; ½ teaspoon ginger; 4oz caster sug 2oz crystallized ginger, chopped; ½ teaspoon salt; 4oz butter margarine; 8oz rhubarb, coarsely chopped; 2 eggs, well beaten.

Sift flour, salt and ginger together and rub in the fat until mixture resembles fine breadcrumbs. Add sugar, rhubarb a crystallised ginger. Stir in the eggs until well blended. Spoon mixt into a well-greased 2 pint pudding mould. Cover with aluminium foil and steam steadily for 1½ hours. Serve with a brown sugar sauce.

Brown Sugar Sauce: Melt **2oz butter** and stir in **2oz brown sugar.** Fold in **2 tablespoons cream.**

If you are not a "ginger" person, substitute chopped walnuts or the grated peel of an orange for the ginger and add to the rhubarb pudding mixture.

SUMMER FRUIT PUDDING

1lb soft fruit, stewed and sweetened to taste; slices of lightly buttered bread.

Line a two pint basin with the bread (buttered side to the basin), pour in the stewed fruit and juice whilst still hot. Place two slices of bread on top; make sure all the bread is well soaked in the fruit juice, cover with a plate and a weight and leave to go cold. When cold turn out into a dish and pour over the pudding a pint of custard. Serve cold.

FRUIT WHIP

3 egg whites; 1 tablespoon grated lemon rind; 2 tablespoons lemon juice; 2 tablespoons of the juice of whatever fruit you are using; cup sugar; 1 cup soft fruit or chopped cooked prunes

Mix all the ingredients except the fruit in a double saucepan over boiling water. If you do not possess a double saucepan a stone jam jar or a jug standing in the boiling water does quite well. Beat until the mixture holds its shape, usually about ten minutes. Fold in the fruit and allow to go cold, or chill in a fridge.

QUEEN OF PUDDINGS

1 pint breadcrumbs; ½ large cup sugar; grated rind of 1 lemon; 1 pint milk; 2 yolks of eggs.

Beat the above together. Put into a buttered dish and bake in a slow oven till set. Remove from the oven and spread top with raspberry jam. Whisk the whites of eggs stiffly, fold in a little sugar, put on top of the jam, and return to oven to brown the meringue.

HONEY PUDDING

½lb self-raising flour; 1½oz butter; ¼lb honey; 1 egg; juice of ½ lemon.

Melt the fat and the honey. Add the beaten egg and the lemon juice. Stir in all the dry ingredients, add a little milk if necessary to make the batter thick. Put into a greased cake tin, cover with greased paper and steam for 1 hour. Serve with sweet white sauce to which has been added the grated rind of the half lemon.

BREAD PUDDING

9-10 slices stale bread; 5oz mixed dried fruit; 1oz mixed peel; 3oz soft brown sugar; 4 teaspoons mixed spice; 2oz soft butter or margarine.

Soak the bread in cold water for at least ½ an hour. Squeeze the bread by hand or in a sieve to expel as much water as possible, then beat with a fork to remove any lumps. Add the remaining ingredients and mix thoroughly. Put the mixture into greased tin or dish and bake in a fairly hot oven for 1½-2 hours.

Sprinkle liberally with caster sugar and serve hot with custard or cold with cream.

Bread, Scones, etc

WHITE BREAD

3½lb flour; 3 teaspoons salt; 1oz yeast; 1 teaspoon sugar; 1½ pints tepid water; 2oz lard.

Put flour in a large bowl, make a well in the centre, place the salt round the edge and put in a warm place. When warm cream the yeast and sugar, mix with half the tepid water and place in centre of the flour, putting the lard in also. Allow to stand in a warm place until it becomes frothy, about fifteen minutes. Make into a dough with the remainder of the tepid water and knead thoroughly. Prove (stand in a warm place until the dough reaches twice the size). Knead into loaves and stand again in a warm place until the dough nearly reaches the top of the tins. Bake in a hot oven, reducing the heat when the loaves begin to brown, for about one hour for 2lb loaves; smaller ones will take less baking time. When ready it will sound hollow when tapped on the bottom. Turn out of tins, cool on a wire tray. (Sufficient for two 2lb loaves.)

WHOLEMEAL BREAD

3lb wholemeal flour; 1 tablespoon salt; 1½oz yeast; 1 teaspoon sugar; 1½ pints lukewarm water.

Place yeast and sugar in a basin containing about 1 quarter of a pint of the water and leave in a warm place for about ten minutes to "prove". Mix together the flour and salt, add the proven yeast and mix, add gradually the rest of the water making quite a wet dough, certainly not one that you can knead, spoon into four 1lb loaf tins, allow to rise in warm place covered with a clean cloth for about twenty minutes, until the dough reaches the top of the tin, then bake in a hot oven for three quarters to one hour. If the loaf sounds hollow when rapped on the bottom it is baked.

NUT BREAD (A very satisfying tea time loaf.)

2 eggs; 1½ cups milk; 3½ cups flour (reserve ¼ cup); ½ cup sugar; 1 cup walnuts; 4 teaspoons baking powder; 1 teaspoon salt.

Mix together the dry ingredients, beat the eggs and add to the milk. Add the liquid to the dry ingredients and then mix in the walnuts, broken small and covered with the quarter cup of flour reserved from the original quantity. Allow to stand in the tin for twenty minutes and then bake in a moderate oven for about thirty minutes. Serve sliced and buttered.

DATE NUTBREAD

12oz self-raising flour; ½ level teaspoon salt; 3oz caster sugar; 1½oz walnuts, coarsely chopped; 2oz dates, coarsely chopped; 2 medium eggs, well beaten; scant ½ pint cold milk; 2oz butter or margarine, melted.

Sift flour and salt into a bowl then stir in sugar, walnuts and dates. Mix to a slack consistency with the eggs and milk stirring well. Fold in melted fat then turn mixture into greased loaf tin, about 4in x 8in x 3in deep. Bake in the centre of the oven at 325°F or gas Mark 3 for one hour. Turn out on to a wire tray. When cold serve with cheese, butter and salad vegetables.

MALT NUTBREAD

1lb self-raising flour; 1 level teaspoon salt; 1 heaped tablespoon brown sugar; 4oz seedless raisins; 2oz walnuts, finely chopped; ½pint milk; 1 heaped tablespoon treacle; 2 heaped tablespoons malt extract.

Sift together flour and salt, then add sugar, raisins and walnuts. Combine milk with the treacle and malt extract and add to flour mixture. Stir well. Turn into a well-greased 2lb loaf tin (or two 1lb loaf tins) and bake in the centre of the oven at 310°F. or gas Mark 2 for one hour, then at 290°F. or gas Mark 1 for a further half hour. Turn out and cool on a wire tray. Serve sliced and buttered.

CURRANT BREAD

2lb flour; ¾lb sugar; ¾lb currants; ¾lb raisins; 2oz lard; 2oz margarine; 3 eggs; 2 tablespoons treacle; 1 tablespoon baking powder; 1 teaspoon bi-carb. soda; little candied peel; 1 pint milk (buttermilk preferred).

Rub butter and lard into dry ingredients. Mix together and bake in loaf tins in moderate oven. Serve in buttered slices.

SPICE BREAD

3 teacups self-raising flour; 4oz margarine or butter; 4oz sugar; 2 eggs whipped; 1 dessertspoon mixed spice; 2oz sultanas; 2oz currants; milk to mix.

Mix the ingredients together to a smooth paste, adding the two whipped eggs last. Place in a well-greased tin and bake for one hour in a moderate oven.

YEAST BREAD

3lb 100% wholewheat meal; 1oz yeast; 1oz salt; 1½ pints warm water.

Put the meal in a bowl and add the yeast and salt dry, crumbled between the fingers. Then add the warm water gradually, pouring with one hand and mixing with the other, until all the water has been absorbed and the dough comes away clean from the sides. Cover with a cloth and stand in a warm place (not over a fire) until the dough is twice its size. This takes one hour. Turn out on to a floured board, shape into loaves, put into greased tins and leave again to prove, until the dough is about two-thirds up the tins. Be careful not to overprove the dough, and keep covered. Put into a hot oven, about 7 regulo 400/450, and bake until nicely brown—about 35 minutes. Cool on a wire tray. Total time, 2½ hours.

CARAWAY BREAD

1¾lb flour; ¼ pint warm milk; ¼ pint warm water; 1oz yeast; ¼lb lard; 2 teaspoonsful salt; ¼lb sugar; 2 tablespoonsful caraway seeds.

Put salt and flour in a bowl. Rub in the fat, add the caraway seeds. Cream the yeast and sugar, add the warm milk and water. Make a well in the centre of the flour and add the yeast, etc. Form into a soft dough, and leave to rise in a warm place until double the size. Form into two loaves. Place in hot oven and bake for about 45 minutes, allowing the temperature to fall slightly.

GLAZED CHERRY BREAD

12oz self-raising flour; 2oz caster sugar; 2oz dates, stoned and chopped; 2 rounded tablespoons malt extract; ½ level teaspoon salt; 2oz walnuts, chopped; 2 eggs; ¼ pint milk; 2oz butter or margarine.
Glaze and Topping:
2oz caster sugar; 1oz walnuts; 2 tablespoons water; 1½oz glace cherries.

Well grease two 1lb loaf tins. Sift flour and salt into a bowl, add sugar, walnuts and dates. Gently heat malt and butter or margarine until the fat has melted. Pour into the centre of the flour mixture with blended milk and eggs. Mix together to a smooth, soft dough. Turn into two prepared loaf tins. Bake for 1 hour in a warm oven at 335°F. or Gas Mark 3. To make the glaze, heat sugar and water in a pan and boil for 2 to 3 minutes until syrupy. When the loaves are cooked, turn out onto a wire rack and brush top at once with glaze and decorate with nuts and cherries.

BELGIAN HONEY BREAD

4½ oz brown sugar; 2 tablespoons of honey; 9oz self-raising flour; half glass of hot milk; half glass of cold milk.

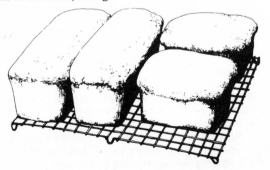

Beat sugar and honey and hot milk. Then add cold milk and flour Bake one hour in moderate oven.

CHEESE AND CELERY LOAF

1lb plain flour; 1 teaspoon salt; 3 large sticks celery; 1 clove garlic crushed, or a few dehydrated flakes; ½ pint milk, less 2 tablespoons 2 teaspoons baking powder; 1½oz butter; 6oz mature Chedda cheese coarsely grated; 1 egg.

Sift flour, baking powder and salt into a bowl and rub in fat unt mixture resembles fine breadcrumbs. Chop celery finely and add t flour with grated cheese and garlic. Beat egg and milk together, ad gradually to dry ingredients and mix to form a soft dough. Knea lightly and quickly on a floured board, then shape into an oblong Place in a greased 2lb loaf tin and bake in a hot oven for abou 50 minutes. Serve fresh with butter.

ORANGE LOAF

1lb plain flour; 1oz sugar; 1oz fresh yeast or 2 teaspoons drie yeast (½oz); 3 medium or 2 large "shells" of orange minced o finely chopped, approximately 6oz (or use 1 whole orange, minced 1 level teaspoon salt (¼oz); ½ pint warm water; 1 teaspoon hone 1 egg.

Mix water and honey in a jug, sprinkle yeast on top. Stand in warm place (about 90°F.) 10 to 15 minutes, or until frothy. M flour, salt and sugar. Add beaten egg, prepared orange and yea liquor. Mix to form a soft dough, adding 3 to 4 tablespoons ext water if required, and knead well until it feels firm. Place dou in a well greased polythene bag or saucepan with lid, and put to r in a warm place 45 to 50 minutes, or until dough springs back wh pressed with a floured finger.

Turn the dough on to a floured board and knead lightly for 1 t

inutes. **Divide into two** and shape each piece into a roll to fit bread
in. Place the shaped dough in a greased 1lb bread tin, and cover
ith a polythene bag. Return to warm place to rise again for approx-
nately 30 to 40 minutes. Bake in a fairly hot oven, on the middle
helf of oven for 30 to 35 minutes. Brush the baked bread with
nelted margarine or butter.

GRANNY'S TEA LOAF

**1lb plain flour; 2oz raisins (stoned); 4oz currants; 2oz chopped
andied peel; 1 level teaspoon nutmeg; 1 egg; 1oz yeast; 1 level
aspoon salt; 2oz butter or margarine; 4oz sugar; ½ pint milk.**

Put yeast into a basin and leave to prove with a small quantity of
pid milk. Mix the sugar, nutmeg, salt and fruit into the flour;
ake a well in the centre and pour in the proven yeast. Add the
eaten egg and the remaining milk, warmed to hand heat. Mix into a
ft dough and leave to rise for half an hour, divide into three pieces
d place in 1lb greased loaf tins, allow to rise until double in size.
ake in a hot oven for 40-50 minutes.

OUR MILK BREAD

o rising required. Bake like a cake.

**1lb wholemeal; ½oz baking powder; 1 teaspoonful salt; 1 dessert-
oonful dark brown sugar.**

Mix thoroughly with sour milk and water mixed, and use a
ooden spoon . Put into a greased tin and bake for about 30
inutes, until well browned in a hot oven. The mixture should be
e a fruit cake and not like batter.

For variety a cupful of rye meal or barley meal can be added and
cupful of the meal (or flour) removed, to keep the weight correct.
Rye meal is very useful in rheumatism, and barley meal has a bene-
ial effect on the kidneys. Both were widely used in the daily
cooking at one time, but people have lost the knowledge of their
good qualities. They are both worth while introducing into the
household cooking.

MILK ROLLS

2oz butter; 1lb self-raising flour; a pinch of salt; ½ pint milk.

Rub the butter into the flour, add salt, and mix with the milk into
a dough. Divide into eight pieces, roll into balls, and make a cross
slit on the top of each, because the surface rises quickly if cut. Bake
on a floured tin and, when partly done, brush them over with a
little milk or egg, to glaze them. These should take about twenty
minutes to bake in a hot oven.

SCONES

**1lb flour; 4oz margarine; 4oz currants or sultanas; 4oz sugar;
milk to mix to a soft dough.**

1lb of flour cuts into about twenty big scones. Two points in the
making the experts insist on are, a really soft dough and a hot oven.
Mix the dry ingredients, rub in the margarine and mix to a dough
with the milk. Roll out about ½in. thick. Cut into rounds and
bake in a hot oven about ten minutes.

BROWN SCONES

**8oz wholemeal flour; 1 teaspoon baking powder; 3oz margarine;
2oz sugar, preferably soft brown; a little milk to mix; a handful of
dried fruit if desired.**

Mix the dry ingredients; rub in the margarine and mix to a dough
with the milk. Roll out about half an inch thick; cut into rounds;
bake in a fairly hot oven for ten minutes.

OATMEAL SCONES

8oz self-raising flour; 1oz fine oatmeal; 3oz sugar; 3oz margarine or dripping; good pinch of salt; milk to mix; 1 egg.

Mix ingredients to a soft dough, cut into rounds about half an inch thick, and bake for fifteen minutes in a hot oven.

APPLE SCONES

2 medium cooking apples; 1 teaspoon salt; 4oz butter; 4oz caster sugar; 1 tablespoon sieved apricot jam; 1lb self-raising flour; 2 level teaspoons baking powder; scant ½ pint cold milk.

Peel, core and finely chop one apple. Sift together flou salt and baking powder. Rub in butter, then add caster sug and chopped apple. Mix to a soft, but not sticky dough with mil Roll out to 8 inch circle, about 1½ inches thick, on floured baki sheet. Mark top into 8 wedges. Peel and core remaining apple a cut into thin slices. Brush top of scone with milk and arran apple slices on top. Bake in a moderately hot oven for about minutes. While still hot brush apple slices with apricot jam. Ser warm with butter.

HERB SCONES

8oz self-raising flour; 2oz margarine; a good pinch salt; 1 teaspoon mixed herbs; ¼ pint milk.

Rub the margarine into the flour, rub in the herbs and salt and mix to a soft dough with the milk. Cut into rounds and bake in a hot oven for about 10 minutes. These are good served hot and buttered or instead of dumplings on top of a casserole.

WALNUT AND HONEY SCONES

1lb self-raising flour; 1 level teaspoon salt; 4oz butter or margarine; 2 level tablespoons castor sugar; 2oz finely chopped walnuts; 2 tablespoons clear honey; approx. 10 tablespoons cold milk to mix.

Sift flour and salt into a basin. Rub in fat with fingertips; add sugar and chopped walnuts, then mix to a soft, but not sticky, dough with the honey and milk. Turn on to a lightly floured board, knead quickly, then roll out to about half inch in thickness. Cut into rounds with biscuits cutters, or cut with a knife; transfer to greased baking trays, and brush tops with beaten egg or milk. Lightly press half a shelled walnut on each scone. Bake towards the top of the oven at 425°F. or gas Mark 7 for seven to twelve minutes according to size.

HOT SALAD SCONES

8oz self-raising flour; ½ level teaspoon salt; ½ level teaspoon dry mustard; 2oz butter or margarine; 2oz strong Cheddar or Parmesan cheese, finely grated; 1 tablespoonful finely chopped onion; 7 to 8 tablespoons cold milk to mix; celery salt.

Sift dry ingredients into a bowl. Rub in fat. Add half the cheese and the onion. Mix to a **soft**, but not sticky, dough with the milk. Turn out on to a floured board, knead quickly and lightly till smooth then press to a round about 1 inch thick. Cut across into 8 to 10 wedges. Transfer to a baking sheet, fitting scones back into round; brush tops with milk and sprinkle with remainder of cheese and celery salt. Bake towards top of a hot oven for 12 to 15 minutes. Serve freshly baked with butter and salad.

POTATO SCONES

1lb boiled potatoes; 4oz plain flour; salt.

Mash the potatoes, add the salt and knead in the flour. Roll out thinly on a floured board, cut into triangles and place on a greased baking sheet. Bake in a hot oven for 10 minutes, turning after 5 minutes cooking. Serve with butter; or fry for breakfast with bacon.

POTATO OATIES

(Makes 12 to 15 Oaties). 1lb mashed potatoes; 6oz fine oatmeal; salt to taste; a little milk.

Mix the potatoes, oatmeal and salt together, adding sufficient milk to make a fairly stiff dough. Roll out about one-eighth inch thick on a floured board. Prick with a fork and cut into rounds or triangles. Bake quickly on a lightly greased heavy frying pan, solid hot-plate or griddle. Serve with plenty of butter.

SCARBOROUGH MUFFINS

1¾lb flour; 1 pint milk; 2 tablespoonsful yeast; a little salt; 2 or 3 eggs.

Warm milk and stir in the yeast; Beat the eggs and add to the milk. Mix the salt into the flour and work it into the milk making a stiff dough. Cut into round cakes. Allow them to rise in a warm place for about 30 minutes. Bake in a hot oven for 30 minutes.

CHEESE MUFFINS

1½ cups flour; ½ cup grated cheese; ¼ teaspoon salt; 4 teaspoons baking powder; 1 egg; ¾ cup milk.

Beat the egg lightly, add the salt and milk, then sift the flour and baking powder together, and put in the grated cheese. Add the liquid to make a dough, beat well and roll out. Cut into rounds, brush with beaten egg, and bake for ten minutes in a hot oven. Eat hot, split and spread with butter.

TEA CAKES

2oz yeast; 6oz lukewarm milk and water; 3lb flour; 2 level tablespoons salt; 12oz lard; 4oz sugar.

Whisk yeast in some of the liquid, dissolve salt in remaining liquid. Sieve flour, rub in lard, add sugar. Pour yeast mixture on to dry ingredients and mix to a sticky dough, adding more liquid as required. Knead well, prove. Knead lightly, divide into round tea cakes and again prove. Bake at 425°F. about ten minutes until golden brown. Rub top of tea cakes with fat when baked.

YORKSHIRE TEACAKES

1½lb flour; ¾ pint milk and water; ½ teaspoon salt; 1oz yeast; 2oz sugar; 2oz lard; 2oz currants and peel.

Put the flour and salt in a warm bowl and rub in the lard, add fruit. Cream the yeast and sugar and add them to the milk, slightly warmed. Pour on to the flour and mix well. Stand to rise for about half an hour. Divide into twelve pieces, roll out lightly, set on warm, greased tins, prick with fork, cover with light cloth and stand to rise for half an hour. Bake in hot oven for seven to ten minutes.

LARDY CAKE

2lb dough (when making bread); ½lb lard; 4oz sugar; 2o currants; 1oz sultanas;

Roll out the dough and spread the lard on it, fold up and knea well. Knead in the other ingredients. Bake in a loaf tin in a fairl hot oven about 1 hour.

SALLY LUNNS

½lb flour; 1 egg; ½oz yeast; ¼ teaspoonful sugar; 1oz butte ¼ pint tepid milk.

Put flour and salt in a bowl to warm. Cream the yeast and suga Melt the butter in the milk and add the beaten egg, also the yeast a sugar. Pour all on to the flour and beat well. Grease three sma loaf tins, put the dough in and leave to rise for 1½ hours. Bak 20 minutes in a hot oven, allowing the temperature to drop towar the end.

Glaze

1 tablespoonful caster sugar; 1 tablespoonful milk.

Mix together and brush over the top of the Lunns when cooke Return to the oven to dry.

FAT RASCALS

8oz self-raising flour; 4oz lard; 3oz sugar; 2oz currants; 1 sultanas; pinch of salt; water or beaten egg.

Rub the lard into the flour and add the other ingredien Mix to a fairly soft dough with a little water, or a little beat egg. Roll out to about half an inch thickness and cut into round Bake in a hot oven for about fifteen minutes till nicely brown.

Cakes, Biscuits and Pastries

BLE CAKE

1. ½lb Judges V., Verse 25 (Last Clause)
2. ½lb Jeremiah VI, 20
3. 1 Tablespoon 1, Samuel XIV, 25
4. 3 of Jeremiah XVIII, 11
5. ½lb 1, Samuel XXX, 12
6. ½lb Nahum III, 12 (Chopped)
7. 2oz Numbers XVII, 8 (Blanched and Chopped)
8. 1lb I, Kings IV, 22
9. Season to taste with II, Chronicles IX, 9
10. A pinch of Leviticus II, 13
11. 1 Teaspoon of Amos IV, 5
12. 3 tablespoons of Judges IV, 19

Beat Nos. 1, 2 and 3 to a cream; add 4, one at a time, still ting; then 5, 6 and 7, and beat again; add 8, 9, 10 and 11, having iously mixed them, and lastly No. 12. Bake in a slow oven hours.

OCOLATE FUDGE CAKE

oz self-raising flour; 1oz cocoa; 6oz butter; 6oz soft brown sugar; gs [blended]; 2oz plain chocolate; vanilla essence.

g:

oz butter; 6oz light soft brown sugar; rind and juice 1 orange; plain chocolate, chopped in pieces; 6oz icing sugar.

Decoration:
2oz plain chocolate.

Sift together flour and cocoa. Cream butter and sugar until light and fully. Gradually beat in blended eggs adding 1 tablespoon of sifted flour and cocoa with last addition of egg. Place chocolate in a small basin and stand in hot (not boiling) water and stir until melted. Cool, then beat into creamed mixture with vanilla essence. Fold in remaining flour and cocoa. Turn into a greased and lined 8in. round cake tin and bake in a moderate oven for about 1 hour 10 minutes. Turn out and leave to cool.

Icing: Put butter, brown sugar, orange juice and rind in a pan, heat together gently allowing sugar to dissolve. Remove from heat, add chocolate and stir until melted. Stir in icing sugar then beat until smooth and a spreading consistency. Split cake in half and fill with a little icing. Spread remaining icing over the top then using a round bladed knife make a pattern on the surface.

Decoration: Put chocolate in a strong polythene bag, tie top in a knot and place in a bowl of hot water. When chocolate has melted, snip off one bottom corner and trickle chocolate in a zig-zag pattern all over top of cake.

MATTER O' MONEY CAKE

1½ cups porridge oats; 1¾ cups self-raising flour; 2oz Scotch moist sugar; 4oz margarine; 6oz cooking dates; a little water.

Boil the dates in sufficient water to make a jam. Mix oats and flour, rub in the margarine and mix in the sugar until the mixture resembles breadcrumbs. Press half the mixture into a cake tin lined with greased paper, spread the date jam over this and spread the remaining cake mixture on top. Bake in a moderate oven about half an hour.

SIX O'CLOCK

This cake was eaten with the early cup of tea before they went to work, by the lasses who worked in the woollen mills.

½lb flour; 4oz butter and lard mixed; 4oz sugar; pinch of salt; 2 teaspoonsful of baking powder (you could use self-raising flour and no baking powder); 1 beaten egg; a little milk.

Rub the fat into the dry ingredients, add the egg and a little milk to make a stiff dough. Roll out about half an inch thick, put on a greased baking sheet, brush over the top with milk and bake in a moderate oven until golden brown. Cut into squares before quite cold.

BEDALE PLUM CAKE

4oz butter; 4oz brown sugar; 5oz flour; half a teaspoonful baking powder; 2oz raisins; 2oz currants; 1oz chopped candied peel; 2 eggs; grated rind and juice of half a lemon; a little mixed spice.

Sieve flour, baking powder and spice together. Cream butter, sugar and eggs together, then add the fruit and the flour mixture. Beat well and bake in a moderate oven for about one hour.

COURTING CAKE

8oz self-raising flour; 2oz sugar; 4oz butter or margarine; 1 egg, well beaten; a little jam.

Rub the fat into the dry ingredients until it is like crum mix to a stiff paste with the beaten egg. Cut in half, roll out o half to about a quarter of an inch thick, spread with jam. Roll the second half to fit on top. Nip the edges together, brush w beaten egg and bake in a moderate oven for about twenty minu

HONEY ALMOND DESSERT CAKE

4oz butter or margarine; 2oz soft brown sugar; 2 level tablespo thick honey; 6oz self-raising flour (sieved); 2 eggs; 4 tablespo milk.

Grease and line a 7in. round cake tin. Cream butter, sugar honey together until light and fluffy. Beat in blended thoroughly, adding a little of the flour with the last amoun egg. Fold in remaining flour and milk. Turn into prepared tin bake in a moderate oven for 45 minutes. Turn out and cool c wire tray.

Topping and Filling:

3oz butter; 1 rounded tablespoon thick honey; 3oz sieved sugar; 1½oz flaked toasted almonds.

Soften butter and beat in honey and icing sugar. Cut in half and fill with half the butter cream. Put together again cover top and sides with butter cream. Scatter with flaked almo

YOGURT CAKE

6oz plain flour; ½ level teaspoon salt; 11oz caster sugar; 1 x carton natural yogurt; 2 level teaspoons bicarb. soda; 2oz bu 3 eggs, separated; grated rind of lemon.

Icing:

2oz icing sugar, sieved; 2 tablespoons lemon juice; grated ri lemon; fresh lemon slices for decoration.

Grease and flour an 8 inch round cake tin.
Sieve together flour, bicarbonate of soda and salt. Cream butter til soft. Add sugar and beaten egg yolks and mix thoroughly. The mixture will be very crumbly at this stage. Add yogurt and lemon rind and beat well. Gradually stir in sifted flour. Whisk egg whites until just stiff and carefully fold into yogurt mixture. Pour to cake tin and bake in a moderate oven, for 1 hour 15 minutes. Turn out on to a cooling tray.

ing: Mix icing sugar with lemon rind and juice. Pour over top of cake and leave to set. Decorate top with slices of fresh lemon just before serving. This cake is nicer when eaten the following day.

OGGY

¾lb flour; 1½ teaspoons baking powder; 2oz lard; 4oz margarine; z golden syrup; 4oz sugar; (or 2oz treacle and 6oz sugar); pinch of salt; milk to mix.

Mix the flour, salt and baking powder and rub in the fat. Melt the syrup and sugar, but don't make it hot; add to the other ingredients and mix to a stiff dough with milk. Roll out about half inch thick and bake on a greased tin in a moderate oven for about twenty or thirty minutes, until a pale golden brown. Cut into squares before cooling.

UNCHY FRUIT SQUARES

nchy Pastry:

z plain flour; 1 dessertspoon caster sugar; 2oz walnuts very finely pped; about 6 tablespoons cold water; ¼ level teaspoon salt; each margarine and cooking fat.

ing: 1lb fruit mincemeat

ift flour, salt and caster sugar into a bowl. Rub in fats until ture resembles fine breadcrumbs, add walnuts then mix to a stiff past with the cold water. Turn out on to a floured board, knead quickly till smooth then divide in two. Roll out each piece into a rectangle, approximately 9in. x 12in. (or a little smaller than your baking tray) and put one on to a greased baking tray. Spread with fruit mincemeat to within ½in. of edges, moisten edges with water then cover with remaining pastry. Press edges together to seal then knock up with the back of a knife. Bake towards top of a moderately hot oven, for 30 minutes or till pale gold. Cut into squares while still warm and dust tops with sieved icing sugar.

DATE COOKIES

4oz rolled oats; 8oz plain flour; 6oz chopped dates; 1 teacupful water; 3oz caster sugar; 5oz butter (melted); 2oz chopped walnuts.

Put sugar, oats and flour into a bowl. Add the melted butter and mix to a crumbly mixture. Put dates, nuts and water into a pan and cook for a few minutes until soft enough to spread. Put half the crumbly mixture into a Swiss Roll tin, cover with the date mixture and sprinkle the remainder of the crumbs on top. Press down well and bake in a moderate oven about 45 minutes. Cut into fingers and cool.

WHOLEMEAL GINGER BREAD

¾lb wholemeal flour; 4oz margarine; 1 teaspoon ground ginger; 1½ teaspoons baking powder; 6oz sugar (soft brown for preference); 2oz treacle; 1 egg, well beaten; a little milk.

Melt the fat, sugar and treacle, mix together the dry ingredients and add the melted fat, etc. Stir well and add the beaten egg and sufficient milk to make a soft mixture. Pour into a shallow tin about seven inches square, well greased or lined with greased paper, and bake for about three quarters of an hour in a moderate oven.

PRUNE SQUARES

Filling: 24 large prunes (approx. 8oz); 2oz butter; 1oz soft brown sugar; ½ level teaspoon cinnamon; 1 level teaspoon finely-grated lemon rind.

Cover prunes with water, bring to boil and simmer for thirty minutes. Drain, cool and remove stones. Cream rest of ingredients together, and use to stuff prunes. Leave in a cool place while preparing pastry.

Pastry: 1lb plain flour; ½ level teaspoon salt; 2oz icing sugar; 4oz each margarine and cooking fat; 5 to 6 tablespoons cold water; 1 egg, beaten.

Sift dry ingredients together. Rub in fats. Mix to a stiff do with cold water. Knead lightly till smooth. Divide in two, mak one half slightly larger than the other. Roll out smaller piece i twelve inch square. Brush with egg. Top with rows of prunes. out remaining pastry into a thirteen inch square and carefully p over the prunes. Press edges well together to seal, then press d firmly between prunes. Cut into squares. Ridge edges with f Transfer to greased baking trays and brush with beaten egg. B towards top of oven at 425°F or gas Mark 7 for fifteen to twe minutes. Cool. Dust with sieved icing sugar before serving.

HOCOLATE OATIES

6 tablespoonsful porridge oats; 6 tablespoons self-raising flour; 2 margarine or butter; 2 tablespoons golden syrup; ¼ teaspoon xed spice; ¼ teaspoon ground ginger; 1 well-beaten egg; 3oz oking chocolate.

Rub margarine into flour and oats. Add sugar, spice and ginger; en well mixed add syrup and beaten egg, and knead until a able paste. Roll out thinly on a floured board, and cut into shapes. e well-greased baking sheets and bake in a moderate oven about minutes until well-browned. When cold, melt the chocolate d sandwich biscuits together. Decorate with a little chocolate on .

NGER BISCUITS

oz self-raising flour; 2oz margarine; 2oz soft brown sugar; teaspoon ground ginger; 1½ tablespoons golden syrup.

Melt syrup, margarine and sugar, add to the flour and ginger and thoroughly, adding a little more flour if too thin. Roll out ly, cut into rounds, place on well greased baking sheets and bake moderate oven 15 to 20 minutes.

TTY CRUNCHES

oz plain flour; 8oz sugar; 4oz margarine; 1 cup porridge oats; up desiccated coconut; 1 tablespoon golden syrup; 1 teaspoon arb soda dissolved in 2 tablespoons warm water.

Melt together syrup, sugar and margarine. Add dry ingredients, in the water and bi-carbonate soda. Place in teaspoonsful on a -greased baking sheet and bake in a moderate oven for 15 0 minutes.

BRANDY SNAPS

2oz flour; 2oz sugar; 2oz butter or margarine; 2 tablespoons golden syrup; 1 level teaspoon dried ginger; 1 teaspoon brandy; ¼ teaspoon grated lemon rind.

Melt the fat, sugar and syrup in a pan. Add other ingredients and mix well. Drop in teaspoonfuls on a greased baking sheet at least three inches apart. Bake in a moderate oven for seven to ten minutes until golden brown. Leave baking sheet to cool on stove top until the biscuits can be lifted with a knife. Roll the biscuits round a wooden spoon handle and leave for a minute to set.

COFFEE CRUNCHES

2oz butter; 3oz caster sugar; 1 egg yolk; 6oz self-raising flour; 1 tablespoonful instant coffee; milk to mix.

Cream the butter and sugar together. Beat in the egg yolk and stir in the sieved flour and coffee. Knead the mixture together, adding a little milk if necessary. Roll into small walnut-sized balls and place on a greased baking sheet. Bake in a moderately hot oven for about 15 minutes.

ELIZABETHAN FLAN

Filling: 2 large thin-skinned oranges; 2 tablespoons honey; ¼ pint water; ¼ pint double cream; 2oz sugar.
Pastry: 6oz plain flour; pinch salt; 3oz butter; 2oz caster sugar; 1 egg yolk; 2 teaspoons water.

(Filling). Wash oranges and cut into thin rings, the peel should be kept on. Soak overnight in honey and water. Next day place oranges in a pan and simmer gently for 25 to 30 minutes. Drain and cool, reserving syrup.

Pastry: Sift together flour and salt, rub in butter until mixture resembles fine breadcrumbs, add sugar. Bind together with egg yolk and water to form a firm dough. Roll out and use to line an 8 inch fluted flan ring. Fill centre with greaseproof paper or tinfoil and baking beans. Bake "blind" in a moderately hot oven for 15 minutes, remove greaseproof paper and beans and continue baking for 5 minutes, until pale golden in colour. Cool. Whip cream until just stiff then spread on bottom of flan case. Overlap orange slices on top. Add sugar to ¼ pint honey juice and heat gently until sugar has dissolved. Bring to boil and cook until syrupy consistency, about 3 to 5 minutes. Use this to glaze oranges and pastry. Serve chilled.

PEACH FLAN

For the case you will require a short sweet pastry made as follows:
4oz plain flour; 2oz corn flour; 3oz margarine; ½oz castor sugar; 1 egg yolk; water.

Mix the flour and cornflour and rub in the fat until the mixture resembles fine breadcrumbs. Stir in the sugar, hollow out the centre of the mixture and drop in the egg yolk. Mix to a stiff dough, adding water as needed. Roll out on a floured board. Line a flan ring or shallow tin, prick the base of the pastry well and bake in a hot oven about 20 minutes or until a pale brown. Remove from oven and leave to cool.

The Filling: Three or four fresh peaches or a large tin of sliced peaches, 4 tablespoonsful apricot jam.

Slice fresh peaches or drain the juice off it using tinned ones. Arrange on pastry case, neatly overlapping the fruit. Heat jam in a pan, sieve, then brush lightly over the fruit and pastry. Decorate with whipped cream.

RASPBERRY AND CREAM ROLLS

Sponge: 3 large eggs; 3oz castor sugar; 3oz self-raising flour.
Filling: 1lb raspberries; 1oz castor sugar; ½ pint double crea lightly whipped.

Grease and line a 9in. x 13in. swiss roll tin. Take eggs at ro temperature and whisk with sugar until mixture is light and crea and whisk leaves a trail when lifted out of the mixture. Fold in si flour, using a metal spoon. Turn into prepared tin and level. Bak a moderately hot oven, for 7-10 minutes until sponge begins shrink from edges of tin and is pale golden brown. Turn out o a sheet of greaseproof paper dredged with castor sugar and t edges of sponge. Lay rolling pin along length of sponge and w round. Leave until cool. Cut into 8 and stand each roll in a pa case.

For Filling: Keep half the raspberries for decoration, remaining in sugar, then fold into whipped cream. Fill rolls w cream and decorate top with a circle of raspberries.

STRAWBERRY SHORTCAKE

8oz self-raising flour; 3oz sugar; 4oz butter; ¼pint milk; 1lb f strawberries; 2 tablespoons castor sugar; ½ pint double cre lightly whipped; pinch of salt; rind of one lemon; 2 egg yo juice of ½ lemon; 2oz butter.

Sift flour, salt and sugar together. Work in butter and lemon using a knife. Add eggs, a little at a time then gradually add milk, stirring, until the mixture holds together, but is still soft. into a lined, greased and floured 8in. square cake tin and bake 10 to 15 minutes in a hot oven. Cool. Cut strawberries in half.

Split shortcake in half and fill with half the strawberries cream. Spread top with remaining cream and arrange strawbe on top. Serve freshly made.

MON MERINGUE PIE

ne an 8 in. flan ring or a deep pie plate with **6oz shortcrust**
ry. Prick all over with a fork. Bake for 15 minutes in a hot
until set. Remove and cool. Blend **1¼ oz cornflour**, **½ teaspoon**
and a little milk taken from 1 pint, bring remaining milk to
pour slowly on to cornflour, stirring. Pour into pan, cook gently
mixture thickens and boils. Remove from heat, stir in **2oz**
. Beat **2 egg yolks** into cornflour, stir in **juice and grated rind**
ge lemon and **1oz butter**. Cool, pour into pastry case. Whisk
whites until stiff, add **2oz granulated sugar**, whisk until
ure is stiff again. Fold in **2oz castor sugar**. Cover filling with
ngue, piling high. Bake in a slow oven until crisp—about
inutes.

ANGE CHEESE-CAKE

z plain flour; pinch salt; 5oz butter; 2oz castor sugar; 1 egg
; 1½ teaspoons water.
ling: 8oz cottage cheese; 1 egg and 1 egg white; 1oz cornflour;
castor sugar; rind and juice of 1 orange; 4oz double cream.
eve flour and salt. Rub in butter until mixture resembles bread-
bs. Add sugar and bind pastry together with one egg yolk
ded with water. Chill if necessary. Roll out threequarters of the
ry and line a 8/9-inch flan ring standing on a baking sheet.
rve the remaining pastry to make a lattice topping.
eve cottage cheese. Blend whole egg and egg white with
flour. Add rest of filling ingredients and mix well. Turn mixture
flan case. Bake in a hot oven for 10 minutes, until filling begins
t. Remove from oven and arrange lattice of pastry on top of
Return to the oven and bake for a further 35 minutes in a warm
, until pale golden brown. Serve cold.

CHERRY MERRY-GO-ROUND

4oz self-raising flour; 4oz margarine; 2 eggs; 2 level teaspoons
cinnamon; 4oz castor sugar; 1 tablespoon milk.

Filling and Topping: black cherry jam or bramble jelly; fresh
cherries; whipped fresh cream or butter cream.

Sift flour with cinnamon. Cream fat and sugar together till light
and fluffy, then add the eggs, one at a time, beating thoroughly
after each addition. Fold in half the quantity of flour, add milk then
fold in rest of flour. Turn mixture into a 7 inch round cake tin, well
greased and line with greaseproof paper. Bake in the centre of a
medium oven 40 to 45 minutes. Turn out on to a wire tray. When
cool cut cake into one or two layers and sandwich together liberally
with black cherry jam or bramble jelly. Spread cream thickly over
the top and decorate with rings of stoned cherries.

Jams, Jellies and Preserves

HINTS ON JAM MAKING

Choose fruit that is fresh, ripe and firm, and a good-sized strong pan, allowing plenty of room for the jam to cook without risk of boiling over. Add the water and cook slowly until tender. Stir occasionally. Add the sugar to the softened fruit and stir until dissolved. Boil rapidly until set, stirring occasionally. When using stoned fruit, remove as many stones as possible when they rise to the surface.

After boiling for about 10 minutes test for setting. Put a little jam on a cold plate and leave for a few minutes. If it is set, the jam will wrinkle when pushed with the finger. Remove the scum from the top. Allow to cool slightly and put into warm, dry jars.

The following table gives the amount of water and sugar required for various fruits:

Fruit	Water	Sugar
Blackcurrants	½ pint to 1lb fruit	1lb to 1lb fruit
Damsons	¼ pint to 1lb fruit	1lb to 1lb fruit
Gooseberries	¼ pint to 1lb fruit	1lb to 1lb fruit
Plums	¼ pint to 4lb fruit	¾ to 1lb to 1lb fruit
Raspberries	None	¾ to 1lb to 1lb fruit
*Strawberries	None	¾ to 1lb to 1lb fruit

*Strawberries need the addition of the juice of half a lemon to 1lb fruit to give a firm set.

APPLE JELLY

Apples; Water; Sugar.

Wash and cut up the apples, add a little water to them in the and simmer for one hour, adding more water should it be neces Strain and allow 1lb sugar to each pint of juice. Heat the juice, the sugar and boil rapidly until setting point.

APPLE GINGER

4lb apples; 4lb granulated sugar; 2oz ground ginger; 3 pints w ½lb preserved ginger.

Make a thick syrup of the sugar and water by boiling toge Peel, core and cut apples into slices and boil in the syrup un becomes transparent. Add ginger, boil another five minutes, b and seal.

BLACKCURRANT JELLY

4 pints blackcurrants; 1½ pints water; Sugar.

Wash the fruit, put in pan with the water, simmer until te Mash well and strain through jelly bag. Allow 1lb sugar to eac of juice. Warm juice before adding the sugar and then boil ra until setting point.

AMBLE JELLY

Wash and pick over the brambles. Put in a preserving pan and cover with **water**, bring to the boil and simmer very slowly until the juice is extracted from the fruit. Pour through a jelly bag and e overnight. Next day put the juice in a pan and add **1lb sugar** ach pint of juice and boil rapidly for thirty minutes or until it when tested. Pour into warm jars and seal.

ERRY JAM

b cherries (when stoned); ¾lb sugar; juice of ½ lemon.
ut fruit, and stones tied into a bag, into a pan, and simmer until fruit is soft. Stir in the sugar and lemon juice and boil rapidly set.

DERBERRY AND BLACKBERRY JAM

rip the stalks etc. from equal quantities of elderberries and kberries, put into a strong pan, bring slowly to the boil and cook 5 to 20 minutes. Allow **1lb of sugar** to each 1lb of raw fruit. n the sugar and add to the cooked fruit. Bring to the boil and rapidly until setting point is reached. Put into warm jars and r at once.

ENGAGE JAM

b greengages; 6lb sugar; 1½ pints water.
ash the fruit, cut in halves and remove the stones. Put the fruit water together and simmer until the fruit is tender. Crack some e stones and add the kernels to the fruit. Add the sugar, bring il and boil rapidly until setting point. Put into warmed jars and

MARROW AND GINGER JAM

2lb marrow (peeled and cut into cubes); juice of 2 large lemons; 2lb sugar; 2 teaspoons ground ginger or 2oz crustallized ginger.
Place the marrow in a bowl, sprinkle with the sugar and allow to stand overnight. Put into a pan and simmer gently, stirring until the sugar has quite dissolved. Add ginger and lemon juice and boil steadily until the marrow looks transparent and the syrup has set.

PEAR PRESERVE

7lb pears; 2 large oranges; 2 lemons; 6lb granulated sugar.
Wash the fruit. Remove seeds from oranges and lemons. Pass the fruit, unskinned, through a mincer. Boil in a preserving pan until clear. Put into jars and cover.

PLUM JAM

4lb plums; 4lb sugar; ½ pint water.
Put all ingredients into a pan, bring to the boil, and boil for 15 to 20 minutes, stirring constantly, and removing plum stones. Test for setting and when ready put into jars and cover.

RASPBERRY JAM

To each **1lb of raspberries** allow **1lb sugar**. Put the raspberries into a pan and bring to the boil. Heat the sugar in the oven. When the raspberries come to the boil add the hot sugar, stir to dissolve it, bring to the boil and boil for five minutes. Then pot up and seal in the usual way.

REDCURRANT JELLY

6lb fruit; Sugar.

Place the fruit and the stalks in a pan and cook slowly until tender. Mash and strain through a jelly bag. Allow 1¼lb sugar to every 1 pint juice. Add the sugar to the juice and stir whilst bringing to boiling point. Boil rapidly for one minute, skimming if necessary, and bottle quickly.

RHUBARB JAM

8lb sugar; 8lb rhubarb peel and cut into inch lengths.

Put into a pan in layers. Sugar top layer, stand for a week, then boil rhubarb and sugar half an hour. Add **1lb citron peel** minced and boil until it sets—about fifteen minutes longer.

LEMON CURD (1)

1 egg; ½lb sugar; 2oz butter; 1 lemon (grated rind and juice).

Put the butter, sugar, rind and juice of lemon in a pan and melt slowly, add the egg, well beaten, and stir until the mixture thickens. This lemon curd will keep six months if butter is used.

LEMON CURD (2)

1lb thick golden honey; 4 eggs; 3oz butter; juice and rind of 3 lemons, good sized.

Beat the honey with a fork, soften the butter just sufficiently to work it into the honey. Beat the eggs and mix thoroughly into the honey. Add the grated rinds and juice of lemons and beat again. Place on a low heat and cook until it thickens, stirring all the time.

MINT JELLY

1 pint vinegar; 1oz gelatine; ½lb sugar; 7 tablespoons chopped mint.

Heat vinegar, sugar and gelatine, stir in mint when practically Re-stir as mint settles to the bottom of bottle.

APPLE MINT JELLY

Wash, remove faults, quarter, but do not peel or core **windfa baking apples.** Put in a pan and barely cover with **equal parts w and vinegar.** Cover pan and simmer till soft (about twenty minu Drain in muslin or similar bag overnight. Measure juice and p pan with **1lb sugar to each pint of juice.** Allow sugar to diss and then boil rapidly in uncovered pan until setting point is reac

Add **1 tablespoon finely-chopped mint to each pint of juice u** for the last minute of boiling. Allow to thicken before bottlin warm jars (otherwise the mint will rise to the top of the jar).

The muslin bag must not be squeezed or the jelly will be clo but if you care to experiment by boiling the used apples with vinegar and water and squeezing, more juice can be obtained a **teaspoon of powdered gelatine** would help in setting it.

APPLE CHUTNEY

7lb green apples; ½lb seedless raisins; ¼lb bruised gi ½lb onions; 1oz mustard seeds; 6 or 8 figs; 2lb sugar [b preferred]; 1lb sultanas; 2oz garlic; 4oz salt; 1oz ci 1/8oz horseradish; 1½ quarts best malt vinegar.

Mix all fruits and vegetables and add to the vinegar. Sin slowly for forty minutes, stirring occasionally. Bottle and tightly.

GOOSEBERRY CHUTNEY

3lb gooseberries; ¼oz mustard seed; 1¾lb brown s ¼ teaspoonful turmeric; ½lb stoned raisins; 4 onions; 2

lespoonsful salt; ½ teaspoonful cayenne; 1½ pints vinegar.
Tie the mustard seed in muslin. Put all the ingredients in an
minium pan and simmer until the gooseberries are pulpy.
move the muslin and bottle at once.

ARROW CHUTNEY

lb marrow; ½lb pickling onions; 6 cloves; 1½lb loaf sugar;
z turmeric; 9 chillies; 1½oz ground ginger; 1½oz mustard;
vinegar; salt.
Cut the marrow into small squares (about half an inch), lay on a
and shake salt over. Leave overnight, then drain. Boil the
er ingredients for ten minutes, then add the marrow and boil for
an hour, or until tender. Put into jars.

UBARB CHUTNEY

lb chopped rhubarb; 2 medium-sized onions chopped; 2 tea-
ons curry powder; 10 tablespoons vinegar; 1 teaspoon salt;
easpoon pepper; 2 tablespoons Demerara sugar.
ut all ingredients into a pan. Cook slowly until soft, then boil
dly till thoroughly cooked. Put into jars.

MATO CHUTNEY

b green tomatoes; ½lb granulated sugar; ½oz red chillies; Juice
lemons; 3 pints vinegar; 4lb apples; 1lb shallots; 3oz salt;
ultanas; ¼oz whole ginger.

Boil vinegar and sugar to a syrup. Tie ginger and chillies in
muslin. Put all the rest of the ingredients through a mincer and add
them with the lemon juice and salt to the syrup. Simmer very gently
for 4 hours. Remove the muslin, and bottle.

BLACKBERRY KETCHUP

Simmer blackberries in just enough water to cover them until
quite soft—about half an hour. Sieve, using a hair or nylon sieve.
Measure the pulp and to each pint allow approximately ½ teaspoon salt, 4oz sugar, ¼ teaspoon ground mustard seed, 1/8 teaspoon ground cinnamon, ½ teaspoon ground cloves, 1/8 teaspoon
ground nutmeg and ½ pint vinegar. Simmer all together till the
consistency of a thick sauce. Bottle and finish.

PICCALILLI

2 cauliflowers; 2 medium-sized cucumbers; ½lb French beans;
1 marrow (not too large); 1 medium-sized onion; 1 quart vinegar;
1oz whole spice; ¼lb Demerara sugar; ½oz ground ginger; 1oz
mustard; ½oz turmeric; 1 tablespoon flour.
Cut the vegetables into small pieces, lay on a dish and sprinkle
with salt and leave for twelve hours. Drain off the liquid. Boil the
vinegar with the spice, except for a little to be used for mixing the
rest of the ingredients to a paste, and strain. Mix this paste with the
boiled vinegar, pour into a preserving pan, add the vegetables and
boil for fifteen minutes.

Wines and home-made drinks

APPLE CIDER

4lb green apppes; 2 gallons water; 2lb sugar; 2oz root ginger (bruised); grating of nutmeg.

Shred apples, cover with water in earthenware bowl. Leave for seven days; strain; bruise ginger; tie in muslin bag and put in strained liquid together with sugar and nutmeg. Cover and leave for twenty-four hours; strain and bottle. Ready to drink in two to three days.

APPLE WINE

10lb windfall apples; 3¾lb sugar; 1 gallon boiling water; yeast.

Remove cores and bruised parts from apples, chop flesh roughly. Put into a large bowl or bucket, cover with 6 pints boiling water and leave to soak for four days, closely covered with a cloth. Squeeze the pump with the hands and stir and strain off the juice through muslin or jelly bag into another bowl. Dissolve the sugar in the rest of the water over a gentle heat and add to apple juice. Cool, add prepared yeast and leave for two or three days. Turn into a fermenting jar and fit air-lock. Leave to ferment. Rack several times as wine clears; bottle when bubbling in air-lock has ceased completely.

BLACKBERRY WINE

4½lb blackberries; 4½lb sugar; 1oz yeast; 1 gallon water (boiling).

Crush the blackberries, pour them into the boiling water and off the heat at once. While the pulp is still hot, strain through muslin and then put the juice through a jelly bag. Bring the strained juice to boiling point and simmer for two minutes. the hot liquid over the sugar and stir until all the sugar is dissol Allow the brew to cool, sprinkle the yeast on top and stir in. C and ferment for fourteen days, then bottle.

BLACKCURRANT WINE

Boil 4½lb blackcurrants in 3 quarts water until all their good is in the water. Strain and squeeze all juice out of the pulp. St again. Boil 1lb rice for five minutes in 2 quarts water. Strain add this to the blackcurrant water. Stir in 5lb sugar. Stir u dissolved. Ferment for one week, keeping covered by a cloth. T strain and bottle.

ELDERFLOWER CHAMPAGNE (a delicious drink for summer days)

2 tablespoons white wine; vinegar; 1½lb sugar; 1 gallon water; 2 lemons; 4 heads of elderflowers.

Put all ingredients, except lemons, into a large bowl; squ lemons and quarter them and add to other ingredients. Stand twenty-four hours, stirring occasionally. Strain and bottle

ew-top bottles. The "Champagne" will be ready for drinking
a few days.

DERBERRY SYRUP

nough berries to fill a preserving pan nearly to the top, with
ficient water to cover; 1oz cloves; 1oz root ginger; ½lb sugar to
h pint of liquid.

lace the berries in the water and boil for one hour, then strain
press out all the juice. Bruise the spices and tie in a muslin bag.
the strained liquid back into the preserving pan with the
uired amount of sugar and the spices. Stir until the sugar dis-
es. Boil for one hour, and, when cold, strain into bottles (a
espoon of the syrup in a glass of hot water is good for colds).

DERBERRY WINE

lb elderberries, stalked; 1 gallon water; ½oz yeast; 3½lb sugar.
rush the washed elderberries in a large jar or bucket and pour
r the boiling water. Cover with a cloth and leave for three days.
in liquid through a muslin or jelly bag into a pan and simmer
a bare five minutes. Cool and add yeast. After two to three days
sugar, pour into fermenting jar, fit air lock. Leave to ferment.
k several times as wine clears and bottle when all signs of
entation have ceased completely.

GER BEER

b granulated sugar; 1oz ground ginger, ½oz tartaric acid;
yeast; 2 sliced lemons; 2 gallons boiling water.
dd sugar, ginger, tartaric acid, sliced lemons to boiling water.
the yeast when liquid has cooled to blood heat, crumbling it
the top. Stir well and leave overnight. Strain into bottles and
lightly. Should be ready to drink in 3 to 5 days.

GINGER WINE

To each gallon of water add **3lb sugar, 3oz root ginger** (well
bruised), **½lb stoned raisins** and the **juice and cut-up rind of one
lemon**; bring to the boil; simmer for one hour, skimming off any
scum; then strain off the clear, cooled liquor into an earthenware jar
or suitable vessel, add **one tablespoonful yeast** (liquified with a little
of the liquor), and allow to ferment in a warm room for a fortnight,
stirring daily; strain off through muslin or filter paper and funnel
into a clean jar or cask, filling full, and when all bubbling ceases,
cork or bung up; it can be bottled for use in four weeks, but
improves with keeping.

NETTLE BEER

Wash well and place in a saucepan **2 gallons of the tops of
nettles**, cover with **2 gallons of water**, add **4lb malt, 3oz hops and
½ teaspoon ground ginger**. Boil this for fifteen minutes, strain and
pour over **2lb of sugar**. Keep liquor at a temperature of about
45°F until sugar dissolves. When cold add ½oz yeast and allow to
ferment. Strain and bottle; tighten corks on second day. Ready for
drinking in four days.

ORANGE WINE

12 large sweet oranges; almost 1 gallon water; 3½lb sugar; yeast;
a little orange rind.

Squeeze the juice from the oranges and make it up to a gallon
with water. Put into a large pan; bring to the boil, add sugar and,
when dissolved, cool and add the prepared yeast. Strain through
muslin into a fermenting jar; fit the air-lock and leave to ferment in
a warm place. Rack several times as wine clears.

When all signs of bubbling in air-lock have ceased completely add
a small amount of orange rind to give flavour to the wine. Remove

orange rind after one day; taste the wine and, if necessary, put rind back for longer. Bottle.

POTATO WINE

Mix **2lb of raisins, 4lb Demerara sugar, 1 pint of clean new season's wheat, and 2 large finely-grated potatoes with 1 gallon warm water.** Add juice and grated peel of **2 lemons, also 1oz yeast.** Allow all this to stand, stirring occasionally, for three weeks. Strain through flannel, then bottle. As soon as the wine is clear, usually in about a month, add **a little sugar candy** to each bottle. It is ready soon afterwards, but improves with keeping.

SLOE WINE

2lb sloes; 1 gallon water; white sugar; yeast.

Remove stalks from fruit, wash and drain. Put the dry fruit into a bowl, crush and leave the pulp overnight. Bring the water to the boil, pour over the fruit and leave for three days, stirring twice daily. Strain through muslin and add 4 lb sugar to each gallon of juice. Stir until dissolved and add 1 teaspoon of baker's yeast to each gallon, creaming it first in a little of the juice. Allow to ferment. Leave for fourteen days then syphon the partially clarified liquid into a clean jar, taking care not to disturb the yeast depo Completely fill the storage jar, cork tightly (waxing the cork he Store for six months in a cold place, syphon off the clear li (filter if required), bottle and cork firmly. Longer storage impr the wine.

MEAD

3lb honey; 1 gallon water; 1 orange; 1 lemon; yeast.

Bring the honey and water to the boil; cool, stir in the juic the orange and lemon and the prepared yeast. Strain through m or jelly bag into the fermentation jar, fit on air-lock. Leav ferment. Rack several times as wine clears; bottle when bubblir air-lock has ceased completely.

TWO-FRUIT PUNCH

1 pint orange squash (ready to drink); 1 pint grapefruit or le squash (ready to drink); A few slices of oranges and cucum Sprigs of mint.

Mix the fruit squashes in a large bowl or wide necked jug. the orange and cucumber slices and mint sprigs on top. Ad cubes when ready to serve. Serve very cold.